King of Hawthorns

The Jeff Astle Story

Glenn Willmore & John Homer

**Perspective
Publishing**

Also available from PERSPECTIVE PUBLISHING

Copyright 2002 Glenn Willmore & John Homer
Frank Skinner foreword copyright Frank Skinner 2002
All rights reserved

The moral rights of the authors have been asserted

First published in Great Britain in 2002 by
PERSPECTIVE PUBLISHING
54 Newhall Street
West Bromwich
West Midlands B70 7DJ8

ISBN 0 9534626 5 X

Concept, book and cover design by Glenn Willmore

Printed and bound in Great Britain by The Bath Press, Bath

FOREWORD

I remember Jeff Astle scoring a goal at The Hawthorns in the late sixties, and, after the ball had hit the net, he went up to the front of the Brummie Road End, I mean right up to the little white wall, and stood with his arms raised. His face and his body language were an expression of pure, unadulterated joy. Kids started jumping all over him (there seemed to be about two million kids at every game in the late sixties.) So many kids climbed on him you could hardly see his blue and white striped shirt. He became half-fan, half-hero. I think he actually put his foot on the wall, thus becoming a bridge between the players' territory and the supporters' territory. It was a moment that seems now to define why Jeff Astle was and is so special to West Bromwich Albion supporters. He was a big star but he was also one of us. You really felt that he loved the club as much as we did.

This is very rare. Long after Jeff stopped playing, I would see him at Albion games, home and away, and when the team scored, I could see that same expression of joy on his face that he had when he stood at the foot of the Brummie Road.

When I was a schoolkid, he was on my wall, he was on the cover of my rough book, I had a blue and white PVC baseball hat with his picture on, and I wore two badges, one of early Jeff with a quiff, set in a blue-plastic star, and another, showing a slightly later Jeff, with a fringe, and that grin. I watched him play for Albion every other week, and I spent the school holidays, hanging around the Spring Road training ground, trying to get his autograph. (I did manage to get it, but only about thirty times.)

It was a strange twist of fate that found me, twenty-odd years later, sitting in a van with a TV crew, heading towards Jeff's house. I was presenting, with David Baddiel, a TV show called *Fantasy Football League*, and we had arranged, largely because of my insistence, to do some filming with Jeff. The plan was to re-create, in Jeff's back-garden, a controversial goal he had scored against Leeds in 1971.

I was nervous. Which is strange because I don't really get nervous. I'd done some very rough stand-up clubs and a fair amount of live TV, and taken it, more-or-less, in my stride, but meeting a hero is a bit different. I couldn't help think that, if he turned out to be a slime-ball, all those things I held in such affection, him at the foot of the

Brummie Road, my Jeff Astle baseball hat, those long hours spent at Spring Road, would all be retroactively spoiled.

But Jeff didn't let me down. He was friendly and funny and really keen to join in, even trying to compensate for our lack of personnel by uttering that immortal line, 'My wife'll be Gary Sprake.' And so she was. I left the house with a signed photo and a grin almost as wide as Jeff's.

When the next series of *Fantasy Football League* was commissioned, we decided to close the show with a regular item, Jeff Astle Sings. It was a smash, with Jeff coming on every week, dressed in an outlandish costume and belting out some inappropriate pop song, as the enthusiastic crowd clapped and cheered along. Once again, he had his foot on that little white wall.

Every Thursday, Jeff would drive down from Burton-on-Trent with his wife, Laraine, and burst into the studio canteen, with a whole new batch of jokes, stories and gossip that he'd heard that week. Every punchline was delivered with a supposedly playful dig in the ribs which, coming from a big bear of a man like Jeff, usually resulted in some minor bruising around my midriff. He was just a big ball of energy and excitement. I'd seen how important he'd been to Albion on the pitch, but I began to realise that off the pitch he must have been something else. I bet he lit-up that dressing room like a beacon.

Anyway, we did a lot of series and we had a lot of laughs. We became friends, and I was so proud to be able to say that. I am even the godfather to his grand-daughter, Taylar. I have some photographs taken at the baptism, with Jeff and me sitting in the garden, chatting away. I remember that conversation very well. He gave me a very graphic description of the strange gurgling sound that Sheffield Wednesday centre-half, Vic Mobley, made, just after Jeff had sort-of-accidentally broken his nose. It was one of those moments when, mid-conversation, I would look up and think 'Oh my God, I'm talking to Jeff Astle.' The hero-thing never really went away.

I still remember getting the message that Jeff was dead. I'm not ashamed to say that I cried, and not in that strangled, muted way that men are supposed to cry, but in a loud, teary, breathless way, like I was still the kid in the PVC cap.

Albion were at home that day, and I was glad of it. I needed to be amongst people who felt like I felt. This was family business. Jeff played in an age before TV showed two or three weekly live matches and all the goals from the games. To see Jeff's work you had to go to see him in the flesh. Only people who watched Albion regularly in the late-sixties and early-seventies, knew how good Jeff was. He was a truly local hero. And when I got out of my car and walked towards the ground, you could taste the grief in the air.

Anyway, I can't write a piece about Jeff Astle and not end on a laugh. He wouldn't like it. I suppose this story sums up Jeff just as much as that image of him at the little white wall.

Generally speaking, the one thing that non-Albion fans know about Jeff Astle's playing career is that he missed a sitter against Brazil in the 1970 World Cup. Clearly, it's outrageous that a great goalscorer like Jeff should be remembered for a miss, but it never seemed to bother him in the slightest. In fact, he delighted in telling the story of how he and another player had shared a cab with two drunken women, some years later. I won't go into too much detail, but the story ends with one of the women saying 'Have you ever felt one of these before?' And Jeff saying 'Yeah, when I missed that sitter against Brazil in 1970.'

Frank Skinner
August 31 2002

Jeff Astle will always be one of West Bromwich's favourite sons, even though he only lived in the town for ten years. To anybody growing up there thirty or forty years ago, as I did, the name Astle was synonymous with West Bromwich. He was the most famous person connected with the town; amongst Albion supporters he was revered in a way that modern footballers never will be. If you went to see the Albion and Jeff was missing from the side, as he was too often near the end of his time at The Hawthorns, you felt cheated, because Jeff **was** West Bromwich Albion for more than a decade. For six or seven years, the entire pattern of play of the first team was organised around Jeff, because of his unique heading ability. A truly great player, and a great man off the pitch. This is Jeff's story; we will not see his like again.

Glenn Willmore

Jeff Astle was an ordinary bloke with a great talent. He scored the winning goal in an FA Cup Final and played for England in the World Cup. He was brilliant in the air – but he always kept his feet firmly on the ground. Despite his fame and the adulation he received, I think he always realised how lucky he was, playing the game that he loved. He also knew what it was like to be a fan. He knew what West Bromwich Albion means to its supporters.

I idolised him. My own favourite memory of Jeff is the hat-trick he scored against Manchester United, in that fabulous 6-3 win in 1968. That evening, under the Hawthorns floodlights he was majestic. I shall never forget it.

Jeff's ultimate gift was his rapport with the fans. He always had time for us – he never forgot us, and loved us as much as well all loved him. This book tells the story of his life. When you have read it you will know why Jeff Astle always was, and always will be, The King.

For my Dad, who turned me into a fanatic

John Joseph Homer

Acknowledgments
We would like to thank everybody who helped with this book. Most of all, the great man, Jeff Astle, himself, for the numerous interviews he gave over the years to *The Baggies* newspaper, Laraine, Ken and Dawn Astle, Frank Skinner, Barry Fry, Graham Carr, Tony Brown, Bobby Hope, Dave Matthews, Ernie Williams, Matthew Bytheway and Laura at Avalon.

Eastwood's most famous son...

Jeff Astle was born in the little mining village of Eastwood, in Nottinghamshire, on May 13 1942; on the same street as the village's only other famous son – writer D H Lawrence, author of The Rainbow, Sons and Lovers and, notoriously, Lady Chatterley's Lover. The Astle family was not well off. Jeff was the youngest of four sons, alongside brothers James, Ken and Gary, and he also had two sisters, Margaret and Sue. As if it was not difficult enough providing for six children, the family was struck by tragedy when Jeff's father died in 1945. His mother remarried, and new Dad Eric (always known as Harry) Coakley brought up the family, but, financially speaking, life was a struggle for the Astles in the austere post-War years. As Jeff remembered, it was not just they who were short of money. "No bugger on the street had got owt. With three older brothers, I always wore hand-me-downs."

At times he would have to go to school in his mother's boots, and in later years Jeff would explain to his three young daughters that that was responsible for the strange shape of his toes! That applied at the seaside as much as anywhere else. As a child Jeff loved the annual holiday fortnight by the seaside of Mablethorpe, in Lincolnshire. He and Gary, the nearest brother to him in age, used to spend their precious tanner in the slot machines on the sea front, but when it came to swimming in the sea, the young Jeff cut quite a startling figure. "We couldn't afford a proper swimsuit. I would have to wear my mother's jumper, with the neck sewn up, and the sleeves cut out to make room for my legs. The whole thing was held up with a snakebelt. It was great until I went into the sea, when the the wool dropped as it soaked up the seawater. When I came out of the

On the beach at Mablethorpe. clockwise from left, Mum Edith, Jeff, James, wife Ruth, baby Susan, Gary, Margaret, Ken

7

sea, it was like dragging a trawler net behind me. It would be full of sand, shells, starfish and dog-ends!"

Significantly, the one article of clothing that Jeff did not have to share was his precious football boots – because he was the only one of the four boys to excel at the sport, although not to the extent that he attracted a host of scouts to watch him, in his early years at least. At ten he was the captain of Devonshire Drive Junior School in Eastwood. When he became famous with the Albion, many years later, Eastwood published a little booklet extolling the qualities of the village, trumpeting it as the birthplace of Lawrence – and recorded that as a ten year old, Jeff scored eighteen goals for his school side in a 22-0 victory.

Jeff's first football mentor – apart from his oldest brother James, who used to transport him everywhere a game of football was to be had – was his sportsmaster at Devonshire Drive, Tom Morley. Such was the coaching and encouragement that he got from Mr Morley that before he left Devonshire Drive for Secondary school, Jeff was rewarded by being selected for West Notts Junior representative side. "And Mr Morley presented me with a big bowl of sweets." As James said at the time, "Jeff just shone. Even at a really young age you could see that he was miles better than everybody else – even when he was playing in boots which were two sizes too small, or two sizes too big."

At Walker Street Secondary School, in Eastwood, Jeff's burgeoning football career moved up another notch when he played for the West Notts Senior Boys team. At 14 headmaster Jack Sprittlehouse arranged Jeff a trial

Jeff, left, as angelic choirboy — aged nine, with brothers Ken and Gary

with Notts County – Jeff's "local" side, and the one he had watched from the Meadow Lane from a very young age. Jeff played in a trial match at Meadow Lane under the watchful eye of the County manager, Tommy Lawton and did well – well enough for County to sign him on amateur forms two days before he reached his 15th birthday. Coventry City wanted him as well, but his father, and his headmaster, after having taken him on trial at Highfield Road, pushed him towards the local side. Once signed with County, he played for the club in the Midland Midweek League, and trained at

Meadow Lane on every Tuesday and Thursday evening.

By now, of course, Jeff had left school, and was heading for a career in the local pits, as his father had. He was an apprentice fitter at Eastwood Colliery, which involved a couple of trips down the mines – usually at Ilkeston Colliery – at least twice a week. It was not a life Jeff relished. "I wasn't a success. In fact, I was hopeless at the job."

In the evenings Jeff persevered with his football, and after a series of good games for the Notts County Colts side, he was taken aside by Lawton and offered a job with the County groundstaff, where he joined a number of players who would subsequently make it big with other clubs, Tony Hateley, Dick Edwards and Terry Wharton. In footballing terms, being a groundstaff lad was hard work – training after the full-time professionals, and cleaning their boots, keeping the stadium in good order, and assisting the groundsman – but compared to working down the pits, it was heaven for Jeff.

Jeff was also fortunate that he was being coached by the great Tommy Lawton, who was the most influential figure in Jeff's early professional career. Lawton had started his career with Burnley before moving to Everton in 1936. There he played alongside the great Dixie Dean.

"Dean was the greatest header of a ball I have ever seen," remembered Lawton, who soon developed a similar reputation in the air, learning, as it were, at the feet (and the head) of the master. Lawton went on to play for England, until the Second World War interrupted his career. He moved to Chelsea before causing a sensation by signing for a record fee for little Notts County in November 1947, before moving into management at Brentford (where, bizarrely, he "sold" himself to Arsenal, and spent four years as a player in the limelight at Highbury before becoming player-manager again, at Kettering. In 1957 he returned to Meadow Lane once more, as manager, and it is no coincidence that two of the greatest headers of the ball in sixties

Jeff, fourth left back row, youngest player in his junior school football team

9

football emerged from his tutelage – Jeff and his colleague Tony Hateley.

Years later, Lawton recalled those early days. "Right from the start I was convinced that Jeff could be a great centre-forward. He had the right build, the ability, and he was quick and willing to learn. We spent hours perfecting his heading, but make no mistake – most of his heading ability is natural. I simply passed on tips about timing and positional sense. It must have paid off, because Jeff reckons he gets half of his goals with his head. But too many people ignore his ability on the ground. He is very quick and he is brilliant at finding the open spaces around goal – the trademark of a top scorer. Jeff has proved season after season that he gets goals even when he is a marked man, and I reckon he now has the football world at his feet."

Twice in those early years Jeff was hit by serious accident and illness. In 1958 horseplay in the County dressing room nearly turned to tragedy when Jeff leapt out of the communal baths when a hosepipe was turned on him, and fell through a plate glass window. With blood pumping from an artery, and his hand near severed, Jeff was rushed to hospital in an ambulance – his young team mate Harry Noon fainted at the severity of the injury. It turned out that Jeff had severed tendons in his wrist, which prevented him straightening his arm and put a stop to his football for months. Indeed, it took many more months of intensive physiotherapy before he could straighten his hand and wrist again.

Just as he regained fitness, he was struck down again. Playing limited over cricket – Jeff always said that cricket was his first love, and he continued to play the game long after his football career was over – for Eastwood St Mary's, he succumbed to pleurisy and pneumonia, and was bed-ridden for several weeks.

However, by the start of the 1958-59 season, Jeff was fit and raring to go.

Jeff (second left, front row), youngest player in the Eastwood cricket club side

At last he moved on from the Midland Midweek League, and progressed into County's third team. By now, Tommy Lawton had left. A disastrous 5-0 home defeat by already doomed Doncaster Rovers in late April helped confirm County's relegation to the Third Division, and on July 1 1958 Lawton was replaced (for the first of three spells with the club) by caretaker manager Tim Coleman, with full-time boss Frank Hill taking over the reins in October, and Coleman remaining as his assistant.

The 1958-59 season was a good one for Jeff, as he established himself in the County Youth side. "In those days I was a left winger. I was rarely considered for the inside trio because, although I was tall, I was as thin as a beanstalk." It was not so good for County. With just one win in their first fourteen games in the Third Division (the first season after the regionalisation of Third Division clubs had been dropped, to create a new Fourth Division) they dropped into the bottom two – where they remained all season. This despite the signing of Roy Horobin from the Albion, who scored eight goals in 27 games, and a debut for Tony Hateley (who made a scoring debut in a 1-1 draw at Stockport.)

Inevitably, cut backs had to be made, as the club dropped into the depths of the Fourth Division – the first of the Football League's founder members to fall so low. At the end of the season, Jeff was called into Frank Hill's office. He was hoping that this might be the long awaited professional contract – he was in for a shock, as was told that, still only seventeen, and yet to make his first team debut, he was being released.

He was not the only one; because of financial constraints, most of the groundstaff were let go, including team mate Terry Wharton, who would later make it big with Wolves. As far as Jeff was concerned, that was the end of his dream to become a professional footballer.

Jobs weren't hard to come by at that time, and within a matter of days, Jeff was in work – working as a dispatcher for one of the biggest companies in Nottingham, John Player, the tobacco giants. To distract himself from the tedium of wrapping and packaging cigarettes and tobacco for export, Jeff started playing for the works' football side; he soon proved himself, playing in successive weeks for the Player's third, second and first teams.

And, as it proved, he had not been forgotten by County. His progress was being monitored by third team trainer Cyril Williamson, and within a matter of months he had an invitation from Frank Hill to come and see him in his office. It was that professional contract. "I didn't need much persuading. I couldn't sign the contract quickly enough; and I was in the Notts County Reserve side the following Saturday."

Jeff made his Football Combination debut against Norwich City, in November 1959, and went on to play a season and a half in County's Reserves, against the second strings of some of the top southern clubs.

11

Meanwhile County's first team were prospering in Division Four, finishing as runners-up behind Walsall at the end of the season. Their run-in was assisted by a superb late finish, in which Tony Hateley, originally a centre-half, was brought in for the last ten games, to chip in, in outstanding fashion, with eight goals.

The side did well back in Division Three, finishing fifth, but slipping out of the promotion race over Easter. The top scorer of the previous season, Bob Forrest, had been completely overshadowed by his young protégé, Hateley, who was top scorer with 27 goals; one year older than Jeff, he was providing his younger colleague with the perfect example of the route to the top of the football pile.

It was while Jeff was plying his trade in the reserve side that he first went out with his wife-to-be, Laraine. Living in the same small village, they had met before. Laraine first remembers shyly throwing a snowball at Jeff – five and a half years her senior – and registering surprise when he coolly brushed the ice from his collar, and smiled back at her.

Things started to become serious in January 1961, when Laraine, aged 15, a lifelong Forest supporter like all of her family, attended a dance with her schoolfriends, in an upstairs room at the local Colliery Welfare club. Jeff – now an established Notts County reserve team player – was sitting in a corner, playing cards with his mates and making half a Mackesons last all night.

He was very shy then – unlike later years – and he sent over one of his mates, 'Jogger' Armes, to ask Laraine if he could walk her home. She agreed, Jeff walked her to her front door – and it was the start of a wonderful romance.

The couple's first proper date was at the Odeon Cinema in Nottingham. In those days the largest cinemas had restaurants attached, and Jeff took the pair of them for a ham salad – Laraine had never been taken to a restaurant before, and she was also Jeff's first girl-friend – before watching the main feature, *The Longest Day*. Laraine recalls Jeff reading a sports news-paper for much of the meal, occa-sionally popping his head over the top to say "Alright love?"

Jeff and Laraine on their wedding day

As the relationship blossomed, Laraine had to address the problem of which Nottingham team to support. "I first saw Jeff play for County at the City Ground, playing Forest in the Notts County Cup Final. I went to the game in my usual Forest colours – I had travelled to see them win the FA Cup at Wembley in 1959 – but I ended up shouting for County, and thinking 'What am I doing?' I never went to the City Ground again after that, except, in later years, when Albion were playing there." The two were married on December 12 1963, at St Mary's church, Gresley.

That County Cup Final was the last game of the '60-61 season, and it is a measure of Jeff's advancement that at the start of the following season, he appeared in the first team squad photograph for the first time, one of eighteen players featured. County did not get off to the best of starts, winning just three of their first nine games, and going out of the League Cup 5-4 on aggregate to Derby County. Hill decided a change was needed, and handed Jeff his Football League debut for the game against Reading, at Elm Park, on September 23 1961. Jeff wore the number seven shirt, had a quiet first outing – and County lost 4-2, with Roy Horobin and Alan Withers scoring County's goals. That was the one and only game that Jeff played for Frank Hill; he was dropped for the next game, a 1-0 defeat at Port Vale, with his best mate – and best man at his wedding — Dickie Edwards taking over his number seven shirt.

Results actually improved after that, with County beating Newport County 8-1, and Tony Hateley scoring a hat-trick in a 3-2 win over Bournemouth, but by the end of October, following a 3-1 defeat by Watford at Vicarage Road, Hill was gone, and his assistant, Tom Coleman, took over, this time in his own right.

Jeff in the Notts County team picture, 1961-62 (second left on the back row)

13

Jeff was given another short run in the side when Bob Forrest was out injured over Christmas, and picked up his first win bonuses when County beat Bradford Park Avenue and Shrewsbury at Meadow Lane.

All told, Jeff made seven League appearances that season, mostly in the number eight shirt, finishing on the winning side only twice, but he failed to find the net once as County finished a disappointing 13th in the Third Division.

Jeff was not in the team for the opening game of the 1962-63 season, a 2-0 defeat against Coventry City at Highfield Road, nor was he in the side when Watford won 3-1 at Meadow Lane five days later, but that defeat prompted Coleman to make swingeing changes for the home game with Bournemouth. There were six alterations in the County side, as Jeff took over the number ten shirt from Tony Flower – and made it his own, remaining in the side for the rest of the season.

This time it took Jeff just five games into the season to get off the mark with his first League goal – the first of so many. It came in undistinguished surroundings, at Colchester's Layer Road, the second County goal in a 2-2 draw. After that, for virtually the whole of his career, the goals would flow freely. He scored in his next two games, in wins over Southend and Bristol City, and recorded his first 'brace' of goals in a 5-0 home win over Swindon Town in the League Cup.

Tony Hateley had been out injured for most of the first half of the season, but he returned to the side just before Christmas, and forged a remarkable partnership with Jeff, the two of them scoring 29 goals between them in the last 25 games of the season, when they were a permanent fixture in the side.

County ended the season in seventh place in Division Three, and Jeff scored a very creditable 19 goals in what was barely his first full season in the first team. Tony Hateley was top scorer, despite missing half the season, with 22 goals, and the two of them were both being touted for great things in the game, as the local and, increasingly, the national press, came to take notice of the goal-scoring wonders at Meadow Lane.

In the summer, Frank Hill left the club, to be replaced as manager by former Villa and Fulham man, Eddie Lowe. His first act was to break up the successful Astle-Hateley partnership, after just 25 games, to sell Hateley to Aston Villa for £20,000. That was the start of a long and lucrative career for Hateley, who, unlike Jeff, prospered well financially from a series of moves to club such as Villa, Chelsea, Liverpool and Birmingham City, but who never really made it to the top of the tree, football-wise, by playing for England.

As a replacement, Lowe bought the free-scoring Terry Bly from Peterborough, to play at centre-forward alongside Jeff, but things were never the same. Bly scored on his debut, a 4-1 opening day defeat at Brentford, but only scored another three goals all season. Without the hard-working Hateley to play alongside, Jeff's play suffered badly too, and he weighed in with just 14 League and Cup goals, which at least meant he was now top scorer – albeit in a side relegated to Division Four, twelve points adrift of safety.

In a season of heavy defeats – 6-1 at Millwall, 5-1 at Peterborough, 5-2 at Shrewsbury – the main highlight for Jeff was his first professional hat-trick, when he scored three goals in a 4-2 Boxing Day win over Oldham. Another first was Jeff's opening goal in the FA Cup; for a man who would one day score the only goal in a Wembley FA Cup Final, it was very small beer – the opening goal in a 2-1 win over Frickley Colliery. By now, Jeff was gaining quite a reputation – a big fish in a small pond at this stage of his career – and he was already a marked man. At times he was lucky to escape serious injury from over-zealous centre-halves. In one game against Doncaster Rovers Jeff thought he had broken his leg, when he was carried off the field by both trainers, after being clattered by one particularly agricultural challenge, but fortunately, after a couple of week's rest his was ready to play again.

At the end of the season, Jeff asked for a transfer; but not because of County's relegation, for he fully accepted his part in that. In January 1963, Jeff and Laraine had married and, as a senior professional by that time, Jeff had been expected to be offered a club house. Instead, he was told that because money was short, the best that could be managed was a rented flat in West Bridgford, with a review at the end of the season. In the summer, Lowe rebuilt the side, bringing in a number of more experienced players – and they ended up having the club houses. "I was furious. I thought County had broken their promise, and I put my case to the chairman, Mr C F Williamson. Eventually I became so fed up, I made a written transfer request."

Jeff the established star at County in 1963-64 (first left on the front row)

To Jeff's surprise, for the request was more of a bargaining manoeuvre, as he thought County were more likely to find their top scorer a house rather than put him up for sale, cash-strapped County, hoping to get another pay-day to equal the Hateley figure, accepted his transfer request, and let it be known that they were open to offers.

On the transfer list at the start of the 1963-64 season, Jeff was on the basic wage of £12 a week, compared with the £25 a week he would have been earning had he agreed to sign a long term contract. With the rented flat costing £5 a week, the newly-weds were not exactly living in the lap of luxury.

Notified of Jeff's availability, a number of clubs were looking at him to see if he had what it took to play at a higher level, as he kicked off the new season back in Division Four. Things were not good, as three times in the first four games County shipped four goals. Terry Bly was dropped after the first game, but Jeff's new striking partner, Bernie Docherty, was no natural goalscorer. In all, Jeff scored just four goals in his first eleven League games of the season, but he added to that total with four more goals in the mid-week League Cup, scoring twice at home to Newport, and twice more in a good win at Torquay.

For some reason, Jeff was having problems scoring on Saturdays – remarkably, all of his seven goals in August and September were scored in midweek games. Which may well have had a bearing on the rest of his career, for he was now being tracked by Albion boss, Jimmy Hagan. Hagan, of course, was busy with the Albion first team on Saturdays, but when he was able, was getting away to watch Jeff – on five or six occasions – in midweek. He must have been impressed with what he saw, but he still had to make the decision whether Jeff was capable of bridging the huge gulf between the Fourth and First Divisions.

Eventually, Hagan made his decision, and contacted County, the two clubs agreeing a £17,500 fee for Jeff's services. Laraine remembers the day well. "I was in the flat with Jeff one afternoon, when I saw Eddie Lowe walk past the window. I shot up and opened the door and invited him in, to be told; 'Quick, Jeff needs to come back to the club now. Jimmy Hagan is here from West Brom, and they want to sign him." Jeff hurriedly left with Lowe, whilst an excited Laraine popped upstairs to tell the Polish couple who lived upstairs that they would almost certainly be moving out very shortly. She had quite a shock later that evening, when Jeff came home looking crestfallen – and still a Notts County player.

Signing for the Albion

In his own words, at that time, Jeff was "young, and at an impressionable stage of life." He had heard on the dressing room grapevine – and from his former team-mate Tony Hateley, for one – about the money to be made on moving to bigger clubs. At that time things were very different to the free-for-all of today's game. There were strict rules about signing-on fees, for instance, but few clubs were averse to giving 'under the counter payments' – 'bungs' – to secure a player's signature. And so Jeff met the hard-nosed Albion boss. Hagan outlined his grand plans for the Albion, and explained where Jeff would fit in, and there was no problem agreeing wages. Jeff would get £40 a week at The Hawthorns, plus £20 a match appearance money, a big jump from his Fourth Division maximum of £25, had he agreed to sign a new contract at County.

Then Jeff made his move. "OK, what's in it for me?" "Nothing," shot back Hagan. "Right then, I'm not signing." And with that Hagan stood up, shook hands, said "Fair enough" – and left, leaving Jeff to trundle back home to give Laraine the bad news. He was convinced that he had blown his chance of a move to a big club, and was mortified. Clearly, Hagan was not a man to be trifled with.

Albion were performing badly at this time. On September 30 they went down to their third consecutive defeat, 2-1 at home to Burnley, to slip further down into the lower reaches of the First Division. Meanwhile, on the same day, Jeff recorded his first weekend goal, in County's 5-1 home home win against Chesterfield, and followed that up with another goal in a 3-1 defeat at Newport on the Monday. That game at Somerton Park proved to be his last in the black and white stripes of Notts County. In future, his career would take on more of a navy blue hue.

Two days after the game in South Wales, which he had watched, Hagan was back at Meadow Lane, bright and early, determined to get his

Albion manager, Jimmy Hagan

man, before he was snapped up by somebody else. This time he brought with him the plain-speaking Albion chairman, Jim Gaunt. There was no messing about, this time. Right lad, what do you want?" demanded Gaunt. "A thousand pounds? Done. You're playing for us tonight!" And with that, Jeff became a West Bromwich Albion player – he would never play for another League club in his career – at 5 pm on Wednesday September 30 1964. This time Jeff was able to return home to Laraine with glad tidings. He went back to the flat with team mate Terry Bly, to pick up his boots and rush over to Leicester, where Albion were playing a Division One game at 7.30. Before they left, Laraine had a quiet word with Bly. "I'm worried. I do hope Jeff is everything they expect him to be." "Don't ever say that. Jeff will go on from strength to strength, and will do really well. Make no mistake about that," reassured Bly. Never was a truer word spoken.

Jeff had profited nicely from the two week delay; and so had Notts County. With two more goals under his belt, and the Wolves, amongst other clubs sniffing around, County decided that perhaps Jeff was worth a little more – and Albion were just that little bit more desperate — and they upped the price to £22,500, which was duly paid.

As it turned out, Jimmy Hagan was to become a big influence on Jeff – almost as important as Tommy Lawton had been. There is no doubt that, as regards Jeff's influence on Albion's fortunes, he was Hagan's best signing. Over time they developed a mutual respect for each other which helped their dedication to the Albion cause. In some ways there is a curious parallel to their careers; well respected and admired at club level, both were heroes in the eyes of their adoring public, but neither received the international recognition that their skills deserved.

Hagan had been a star in Sheffield United's pre-War line-up, but had never been able to command the place in the England team that his silky skills deserved. Taking to management after the war, he took Peterborough United into the Football League with some astonishing goal scoring feats, before moving to The Hawthorns in 1963.

Less than three hours after signing for the Albion, Jeff made his Albion debut against Leicester City, in front of 17,214 at Filbert Street. He and Laraine had driven at top speed across the East Midlands in their red A40, but had trouble in the rush-hour traffic around Nottingham, so when he arrived at the car park at Leicester, he was running very late, and fearful of a first day dressing down from his new boss. When he stopped at the gate, the steward demanded his pass. "If you're a West Brom player, why aren't you on the coach?" "Because I only signed today. Go in and ask who I am." "No, I can't leave here. It's more than my jobs worth..." At that Jeff put his foot down and accelerated through the gates – and if the jobsworth had not jumped back sharpish, Jeff would have driven over his foot. He got out, threw the keys at Laraine, told her to lock up, as the gateman approached, and ran through the players' door, boots in hand.

Tony Brown, for ten years Jeff's main striking partner, can remember Jeff running into the dressing room that day. "In dashes this new man, all of a sweat, wearing grey flannels and a green blazer, with brass buttons up the front. We all thought he was the coach driver for the team bus, because they used to wear the same get-up then! But he soon proved he was a player – and what a player. Afterwards we ribbed him mercilessly and he never wore the outfit again, but it was a great ice-breaker, and we knew we had a real character in our midst."

At that time, Albion were very much in a transitional phase, with several players injured and suffering a loss of form. Hagan, in the job now for eighteen months, was looking for new blood to revitalise the team. Since Ronnie Allen had left the club – later followed by the beefy Derek Kevan – a goalscoring centre-forward had been a priority. John Kaye had been signed from Scunthorpe for an Albion record fee of £45,000, but his early career with the club was dogged by injury, and Hagan had been forced to cycle through a succession of "make-do" strikers of the likes of Jack Lovatt, Keith Smith, Eddie Readfern, Ronnie Fenton and the up-and-coming youngster Tony Brown, who all tried to wear the number nine shirt. Destiny was to dictate that Jeff Astle was the one man who could fill the shirt that Ronnie Allen, Derek Kevan, David Walsh, Freddy Morris and W 'G' Richardson had all worn with such distinction at The Hawthorns.

When Albion lined up against the Foxes under the Filbert Street floodlights that night, they brought with them a terrible record of just one win in their previous ten games, and home attendances had dropped as low as 15,000 for the home defeat against Burnley four days before.

The team at Leicester showed three changes from the Saturday. Jeff lined up at number 10, replacing midfielder Ian Collard, who had made his debut against the Clarets. Back from injury came John Kaye, who, still without a goal to his name all season, wore the number nine shirt, whilst Gerry Howshall came in to replace Scottish midfield maestro, Bobby Hope, who was suffering from a septic ankle.

Jeff had been used to small gates at County; rarely had he ever played in front of crowds of more than four figures. Similarly, Laraine, who used to watch his every game at Meadow Lane, was shocked by the relative munificence of Filbert Street. "Notts County was a homely little club, and it was a real shock climbing up into the main stand at Leicester. It was so steep, I thought I could never get used to it!" She was also confused, once the game got underway, by an Albion fan in front of her shouting 'Come on you Baggies.' "I just couldn't understand it. I'd read that the Albion were nicknamed the Throstles, and I didn't understand who the Baggies were. There I was shouting at the top of my voice; 'Come on you Throstles!' I soon learned that NOBODY in West Bromwich called them the Throstles."

In contrast, Jeff was not at all phased by the big atmosphere, which set his pulse racing in the best possible way. "Far from unnerving me, the tension in the air only served to increase my anticipation of the kick-off."

Hagan, in his pre-match talk, told Astle that he wanted him to forge a partnership with John Kaye, to form a double spearhead down the middle, and to try to take some pressure off the beleaguered Yorkshireman. That would take some time. In the first ten minutes Astle missed a sitter, shooting over from inside the six yard box. As Bob Blackburn, in the *Birmingham Post* noted in his report, "Astle impressed, particularly in the first half, looks pretty good in the air (this was the equivalent of the precis written about Fred Astaire's first screen test; "Can sing, can dance a little") and certainly uses the ball well, and he might easily have scored a debut goal in the first half."

As it turned out, the striking partnership drew a blank, as Albion lost 4-2 and Leicester's recently transfer-listed star, Frank McLintock, was the difference between the sides Jeff did not let the missed chance bother him. He never did. He always looked forward to the next game to make up for missed chances. He never dwelt on that side of things. Most important, he took the view that "I had survived the first big test. I realised that I had the right mental make up to meet the challenge of the pressure and tensions of modern day football."

Three days later, Albion were playing away again, at Sheffield United, and once again Hagan had to ring the changes, bringing on Ray Fairfax, Ronnie Fenton and Geoff Carter, for Williams, Kaye and Clive Clark, which meant that, for the first time, Jeff was able to wear the Albion number nine shirt that he was to make his own.

This time the result was much better. Albion led at Bramall Lane, through Carter, but Ronnie Fenton pulled a muscle, effectively reducing the side to ten fit men, and eventually Albion conceded a late goal to Alan Birchenall. Once again, Jeff was pleased with his contribution. "I felt that I was getting a feel for the First Division."

On Saturday October 10, Jeff was to earn his first win bonus with the Albion. Their visitors to The Hawthorns were Wolverhampton Wanderers, and the Black Country Derby, as it is referred to now – then it was the South Staffs Derby – was usually an exciting encounter. Throughout the 'fifties it had usually been a top of the table clash of national footballing significance, but since the start of the new decade, both venerable Staffordshire clubs had been in decline. That season the Albion had picked up ten points from twelve games, but Wolves were even worse, bottom of the table with just three points, having sacked their great manager of the fifties, Stan Cullis, just a matter of weeks before. What a match to make your home debut.

Only once before had Jeff played in front of a bigger gate that the 23,006 who turned up at The Hawthorns that day – in a third round FA Cup tie for Notts County at Maine Road three years earlier. There were yet more changes in the side, but most significant was the return of John Kaye, who had been injured at Leicester. Wolves' side was a poor patchwork of youth and experience. Only Flowers and Showell

Jeff poses for the camera in 1964

remained from the Wolves side that had dominated the Midlands in the 'fifties. Peter Knowles was a rising star, and Darlaston-born Graham Hawkins was making his League debut – and it was his job to mark Jeff!

This was the game, on an autumnal afternoon in West Bromwich, that would see the start of a love affair between Jeff and his adoring Albion fans, that would last until the day he died – and beyond. The Albion supporters took to Jeff immediately, and he made sure that he never disappointed them in the future.

As early as the 25th minute, the crowd rose to acclaim their new hero. Fred Davies punched out a cross from Bobby Hope, to the feet of John Kaye. He held the ball up long enough for Jeff to step up and open the scoring, and record his first goal for the Baggies. After that, Albion penned the Wolves in their own half for almost the whole of the remainder of the game. They held out until the 56th minute, when Graham Williams' free kick found Clive Clark, who crossed for the unmarked Astle to score again.

With Jeff playing a blinder, they made it 3-0 on the hour, when Williams put in a cross and Kaye – revelling in the space that Astle was creating – smashed home his first goal of the season with a shot from twenty yards.

Five minutes later it was four, when Astle's neat pass sent Clark away down the left, top cross for Kaye to slot home his second goal from ten yards. Knowles scored a consolation goal for a demoralised Wolves, but with time running out Bobby Cram made it 5-1 from the penalty spot. It was Albion's biggest home win against their neighbours for nearly half a century, and proved a disaster for the Molineux men. George Showell played just two more games for the club before bringing down the curtain on a wonderful career – and poor, shell-shocked Graham Hawkins would not play another first team game for more than two years. The Wolves remained bottom of the League all season, and were relegated to Division Two for the first time since 1932.

All the post-match talk was of the impact of the new, raw-boned

The famous 'squashed ball' photograph — the best header of a ball, ever...

22

striker. The *Sunday Mercury* was gushing in its praise. "The Astle-Kaye link-up was the highlight of the match. The two blended perfectly. It was Astle, a tall, deliberate and careful player, who took the game's individual honours. His shrewd prompting and probing and general leadership is just the tonic the Albion forward line has long needed." It was hard to believe that just thirteen days before, Jeff had been playing for Notts County in a Fourth Division game at Newport County. He had looked so comfortable at ease in his new surroundings, that it looked as if he had been playing in the First Division for years. Jeff was content to praise his strike partner, Kaye, who had played on despite getting a nasty knock in the first half. "Yorkie looked an incredible sight as he charged through the Wolves defence. He must have been in considerable pain, although you would not have guessed it!"

The Albion programme, the *Albion News*, for the following week's Reserve game against Chesterfield, welcomed the new man's great start with a prescient comment. "It looks as though Albion's headquarters could become Jeff Astle's favourite ground. We hope so – if he is to score two goals in every appearance here!"

After playing three games in the space of eleven days for his new club, Jeff had time to draw breath after the Wolves game. For a week or two he had been stopping in digs in Dagger Lane, supplied by Winnie Rushton, who had also put up his new colleagues Ken Foggo and Gerry Howshall when they had first come to the club, but then he had the opportunity to arrange a move to the club house that Albion provided for him in Springfield Crescent in West Bromwich, not far from the Albion's training ground in Spring Road.

The house had recently been vacated by Albion's trainer, Wilf Dixon, and one morning Jeff dropped Laraine off at the house, straight from Nottingham, before dashing off to training – leaving his wife to oversee the aggravation of the removal men! It was definitely a club house – the clothes line in the back garden was strung between an apple tree and a real goal post! It was to be home for Jeff and and Laraine for the next six years, which would see the birth of the second of their three daughters, Dawn, in January 1968 – elder sister Dorice had been born in June 1964.

The house was definitely Laraine's domain. When Jeff decided to help out, chaos would often ensue. Like the time he decided to cut down the apple tree – with a clothes-line full of nappies attached, which Laraine saw shooting past the window as the tree came down. Or the garden shed which, Frank Spencer-style, Jeff decided to demolish from the INSIDE, by pushing out the walls, leaving the windows to shatter, as the lean-to came toppling down around him. As Laraine joked, "It was just as well that the football paid the rent!"

Jeff settled into his new surroundings – and made new friends — so quickly. He had that sort of personality. Albion, in those days, was another homely club, just like County, but on a greater stage. Then, all the players lived near the ground, many in Great Barr, and they all went shopping in the town centre, went out to the local pubs in the evening, and really mixed with the fans. When Albion lost at home, the supporters would turn to Laraine, sitting in the stands, and joke, "No tea for Jeff tonight," and she would agree, "No, no tea tonight!" And that was as much as was said.

Back on the training ground, Jeff soon learned what a hard taskmaster Jimmy Hagan was, as he called Jeff in for extra training at Spring Road. Hagan reckoned his new signing needed sharpening up, and put him through some extra training stints which were tough and gruelling – unreasonably so, Jeff thought. New Albion trainer John Jarman would, under Hagan's instructions, have Jeff lapping the track against the clock in the afternoons, when everybody else had gone home. "Sometimes I was so stiff afterwards that I could hardly walk."

Hagan did have his softer side, though, and on one occasion, when Jeff had reacted badly to a cortisone injection, before a game against West Ham. the manager drove Jeff home and – despite his small frame – carried the burly six foot striker upstairs on his back to recover. Hagan was indeed a hard customer.

John Kaye, Jeff Astle and Ray Crawford all wanted that No. 9 shirt!

Back on the pitch, the games came hard and fast in the First Division. Astle paid his first visit to Villa Park, when he played against former County team mates Tony Hateley and Ron Wylie. Albion won 1-0, with a goal from Gerry Howshall, even though Graham Williams had been sent off by referee Jim Finney, for fighting with Villa's Harry Burrows; the following week the Albion captain apologised to the fans through the medium of the club programme – how times have changed. After Villa, it was Liverpool at The Hawthorns. A spanking 3-0 win, and another goal for Jeff Astle.

And that was the end of the honeymoon. Albion – and Jeff – struggled through the winter months. After their win over the Reds, Albion went eleven games without a win, and Jeff played fourteen League games without a goal.

During that almost barren spell, his only goal came in his first FA Cup tie for the Albion. At County Jeff had always been inspired by cup competitions – he scored ten times in twelve cup games for County — as he would also be at The Hawthorns. He always gave that little bit extra when wound up by the magic of the Cup, and he recorded his first cup goal for Albion in a 2-1 home defeat by Liverpool. Roger Hunt and Ian St John scored for the Merseysiders in that third round tie, and the Reds went on to lift the FA Cup for the first time that season at Wembley. Jeff was glad of his fans' support. "During that bad spell I sent a number of shots and headers just wide, or against the woodwork. The fans concealed their disappointment, and carried on chanting my name. Their encouragement helped me get back to form." Not for the last time, the fans stuck with Jeff through lean times.

By the end of February 1965, Albion were in 16th position, just four points ahead of the Villa, who were 21st. These were hard times for the Midlands clubs, as Blues were 20th, and Wolves, of course, were bottom. On the 27th, Albion were at home to Villa in a real "four pointer" as they were called in those days, before three points for a win. Making his home debut for the Albion was England international centre-forward Ray Crawford. Hagan had signed him from Wolves as cover for John Kaye, who, it appeared, has a serious long term injury. It meant that, for the first time in their history, Albion had three top class centre-forwards on their books, in Astle, Kaye and Crawford.

Villa turned out to be "easy meat." Jeff broke his goal drought, to open the scoring, showing his uncanny ability to please his fans in a Derby game, Bobby Cram netted a penalty and Bobby Hope weighed in with the third in a comfortable 3-1 win, as Albion completed a League

"Double" over the Villa for the first time in 76 years of League football between the two clubs. The old order was changing...

With Jeff having discovered his scoring form, and scoring six goals in the last eleven games, Albion scrambled to safety, recording impressive wins against Leicester (6-0, Astle 2) and Everton (4-0, Astle 2.)

After the match against Everton, Hagan, not generally noted for praising his players, was generous in his assessment of Astle. "It may have seemed a gamble paying out a large fee for a Fourth Division player, but I did not look at it like that. I watched him six times before deciding he was ready for promotion. Now that he has matched himself to the faster pace of the First Division he is able to use his best points more successfully." Being 'hard man Hagan' there had to be a sting in the tail. "He could be an even better player if he used more bustle."

Over Easter for the first time Jeff came across a team he would always enjoy playing against, one he would almost always find the scoresheet against; West Ham. On Good Friday 1965, he scored Albion's goal in a shock 6-1 hammering at the Boleyn Ground. It was also the first time that he met Bobby Moore – for whom he would have a lasting admiration and friendship. Brian Dear scored five of West Ham's six goals, prompting the famous headline, 'Oh Dear, Oh Dear, Oh Dear, Oh Dear, Oh Dear!' Three days later the Baggies turned the tables, beating the Hammers 4-2 at The Hawthorns, and Jeff scored again, along with Ken Foggo – and Tony Brown. That was significant, because it was the first time that "Astle and Brown" – a phrase which was to trip off the tongue of Black Country folk as easily as "Lennon and McCartney" or "Enoch and Eli" – had scored in the same game. Part of that game was played in a freak blizzard. It would not be long before, thanks to Astle and Brown – and, indeed, Kaye and Hope, and Clark and Cram – it would be raining goals at The Hawthorns.

Jeff could look back at a promising first season in the top flight. He had played in 33 League and Cup games, scoring eleven goals, to end as joint top scorer alongside winger Clive Clark; an outstanding achievement for a striker straight out of the Fourth Division. At the season's end, the Midlands' soccer Bible of its day, the *Sports Argus* Annual, reflected on Jeff's performances. "Played most of his early games at centre-forward, but showed best form when switched to inside right." It was still a while before the name Jeff Astle would become synonymous with the number nine shirt.

26

Winning trophies

When Jeff joined the Albion he probably did not begin to realise what horizons would open up for him. He was now a First Division footballer at a top flight club, one with great traditions in the game (with all due respect to Notts County, who are, after all the oldest of all the League clubs.) In these days of long-haul package holidays, it is hard to believe that, as at July 1965, Jeff had never been inside a plane. Now he had to, because the Albion had accepted an invitation to play in the prestigious New York Tournament, along with Kilmarnock, Ferencvaros (Hungary) and Bytom (Poland.)

The games were played at the Downing Stadium on Randalls Island, in the stifling heat of a New York summer, and none of the Albion team enjoyed the experience, contriving to lose their last game 6-0 to Byton, so that they could come home early. The first Albion matchday programme of the new season commented on the adventure. "The extreme drought conditions gave us a very bumpy, hard pitch which caused a high percentage of errors on both sides. One thing that the crowds appreciated our side for was the way they put in maximum effort in heat and humidity we frankly had not met before, much less played football in. With such a tight schedule there were not many free days and our lads certainly appreciated the odd occasions when they could get down to the cooler beaches, out of the pulsating concrete streets and avenues of the great city. To make training bearable, the players were out at 7 am in Central Park, when it was a mere 80 degrees."

Hot in New York City; left, on Broadway, right, on the Staten Island ferry

27

Training, even with the concession of an early start, was a sore points for the lads in New York. The Central Park sessions were based on endless running, which made some of the players physically sick, and there was talk of a training strike (shades of 1963), but the players had a difficult case to plead when the 47-year old Hagan generally led the way on these exhaustive runs. Because of the heat, whatever free time the players had was usually spent in air-conditioned hotel rooms, playing cards – with Jeff organising the card schools, of course – but there were some sight-seeing tours arranged, to the United Nations building, the Empire State, the Statue of Liberty, and a night out on Broadway.

On the domestic front, the tour was the first time that Jeff and Laraine had been apart for any substantial time since they had met. Laraine hated the separation. "I could put up with anything else, but I cried all the time because I couldn't stand us being apart for so long. When Jeff was at home, we did everything together, and I used to count the days he was away. Jeff was very much a home bird, and he hated touring as well, and he used to write to me almost every day, really long letters." However, international jet-setting was all part and parcel of being a top football professional at that time, and Laraine appreciated it was just something she – and Jeff – would have to get used to.

For the record, Albion finished third in their four-club group, behind the Poles and the Hungarians, and Bytom went on to beat the New Yorkers, who had won their five-club Group One (which featured West Ham, The New Yorkers (USA), Munich 1860 (West Germany) , Portuguese (Brazil) and Varese (Italy) 5-2 in the two-legged Final. Jeff, home-sick from the start, scored just one of the Albion's six goals, in a 1-1 draw against Ferencvaros.

After the defeat against Bytom, the Albion party left for the airport, almost savouring their long flight back over the Arctic circle, via Iceland. There was one last obstacle, for when they boarded their plane, the flight was delayed on the tarmac for two hours because of air traffic congestion. "It was being locked inside an oven," recalled Jeff, who always hated flying. "We had to sit and suffer because the air conditioning, which operated from the aircraft engines, could not be switched on. It was a hot ending to a hot trip."

Back home in England in August 1965, Albion prepared for the season ahead. In those days, if you wanted to watch the Baggies, you had to go to the match! Televisions were black and white, *Match of The Day* was on *BBC2* (which few people could receive) and *Star Soccer* was still two years away from its debut on *ATV*. If you didn't make the match, and waited for the Saturday evening football results, you would have to suffer Dr. Who on the *BBC* and wrestling (with Kent Walton) on *ATV*.

Who would realise what effect television would have one day on the career of Jeff Astle?

The 1965-66 opened at The Hawthorns with some super football against West Ham, which earned the Albion a splendid 3-0 win, Jeff scoring once to add to two goals from winger Clive Clark, before 19,000 fans. The supporters still needed convincing that Albion would be a serious threat in the coming months, but Albion soon showed their attacking

Moody and magnificent — Jeff the hat-trick man

credentials, with performances which were a world away from the often dour football of recent years.

They started the season like an express train, winning six of their first nine games, blasting in 21 goals in the process – of which Jeff managed ten! His real purple patch came in six days in September, when he went goal crazy.

It has been a long-held myth that Jeff netted three hat-tricks in those six days, but seven goals was pretty good, and the facts are these. On September 4 Sheffield Wednesday came to The Hawthorns. Albion took the lead in the fifth minute of the game, when Ken Foggo crossed and Astle beat his marker, centre-half Vic Mobley, with whom he would have many torrid battles, to head home the opening goal past Springett. Peter Eustace equalised twenty minutes later and, against the run of play, Hickton put the visitors ahead, before Jeff scored another header to level a minute before the break.

A minute into the second half Jeff completed his first-ever Albion hat-trick when he cracked home a pass from John Kaye, and Kaye finished Wednesday off with a fourth goal in the 66th minute.

Jeff was bubbling with confidence – so much so that it turned out that before the game, he had actually told his team mates that he was going to score a hat-trick against Wednesday!

Three days later Albion went north to meet Everton at Goodison Park, where 43,000 spectators saw them beat Everton 3-2. coming back from 2-1 down at half time to win, thanks to goals from Kaye and Astle.

Next up were newly promoted Northampton Town. The match was played on the County Ground on Friday September 10, brought forward 24 hours because of the Northampton Agricultural Show (rather than the requirements of *BSkyB* or *ITV Digital*!)

Hat-trick number one, against Sheffield Wednesday at The Hawthorns

Bobby Hope put Albion ahead after just five minutes, and six minutes after that, Jeff made it two when he slotted home a low cross from Foggo, only for the Cobblers to level by the break. Nine minutes into the second half – with Graham Lovett now on the pitch, as Albion's first ever substitute in a League game – Tony Brown crossed for Astle to score again, and three minutes after that Jeff headed in a Kaye centre to complete his second hat-trick of the week. The home side pulled another goal back five minutes from time but Albion managed to hold out for a thrilling 4-3 win. By the end of a historic night, Jeff was, not surprisingly, the First Division's top goalscorer, and Albion were sitting pretty at the top of the League, for the first time since 1954.

And it was not just Jeff who was reaching top form. John Kaye was still benefiting greatly from Jeff's presence, and he helped himself to a hat-trick in Albion's 6-2 win against Stoke City, and his form earned him a call-up for England, and games for the Football League side, although, unlike Jeff, he never earned a full England cap.

As Albion's surge up the table continued, there was a slight distraction on the horizon, as the club entered the League Cup for the first time. The competition had been introduced in 1960, but had not been a great success, a fact not unconnected with the fact that many of the top clubs – like Manchester United, Spurs, Everton, Liverpool and Albion – had declined to enter. However, Albion, at least, decided to take part, lured by the decision to put on offer one of the League's Fairs Cup places for the winners.

Initially, the draw for the cup was made on a regional basis, and when Albion were paired against Walsall at The Hawthorns, the interest was phenomenal, and a new competition record – bigger than that recorded in any of

Jeff completes his second hat-trick in seven days, at the County Ground

31

the ten (two-legged) Final games played so far in the history of the competition – of 41,188 passed through the turnstiles to witness a classic struggle eventually won 3-1 by the Albion.

On October 13, in round three, Albion faced the awesome task of a trip to Elland Road to face the new force in English football – Leeds United. Managed by Don Revie, they had finished as First Division and FA Cup runners-up in April. Revie's tough and no-nonsense professional approach to the game was to become notorious, but this time he sprang a real surprise by fielding seven reserves in his team, and Albion responded well by racing into a 4-0 lead within the first twenty minutes of the game, with Jeff notching his first League Cup goal for the club. It was the first of nineteen which would see him end his career as the club's top scorer in the competition, one club record which his pal Tony Brown does not hold, and one which is unlikely to ever be beaten.

Jeff, at this point, had not missed a game since signing from Notts County, but in his next game – although he scored the equaliser in a 1-1 draw – he injured his knee, an knock which left him sidelined for the next three League games, plus a League Cup tie at Coventry. Ray Crawford deputised for Astle at High-field Road, but Jeff was back for the replay, and came back in style, despite his dodgy knee, scoring his third hat-trick of the season in a 6-1 win.

He scored his first goal after just forty seconds, when he drove in a Ray Fairfax cross from the edge of the box. Hudson equalised for City, but Tony Brown gave the Albion a half time lead. George Curtis was giving Jeff a real hammer-ing throughout (Jeff came off at the end complaining of 'Curtisitis!'), and was very lucky to escape punishment from the referee, but Astle retaliated in the best possible way, when he headed home a Clark cross in the 58th minute. Two more goals followed from an unusual source – half back Doug Fraser – but Astle rubbed salt in the Sky Blue wounds by heading past Wesson in the 77th minute. The Bishop of Coventry had a close association with City at that time, and it was reported that one of the City staff had asked him for a prayer when his side were under the cosh in the second half. His reply – "It's not God we need; it's Astle!"

Jeff failed to score in the 3-1 win over Aston Villa in the next round at The Hawthorns, but, in a rainstorm, set up a goal for Tony Brown, which sent most of the 40,694 fans home happy, as Albion moved into the semi-finals – and a two-legged tie against Jimmy Hagan's former club, Peterborough United.

Jeff was struggling to get fit for the first meeting, at The Hawthorns, because of his knee problems, but he was chosen ahead of Ray Craw-ford for the game against the Posh, who, in a neat piece of symmetry, were managed by former Albion boss, Gordon Clark. And Clark nearly pulled off an upset with his side of old-timers. To blunt Albion's free-scoring attack, Clark played Vic Crowe as a "fourth half-back" – who still managed to get up front enough to open the scoring in the 16th minute. Tony Brown headed an equaliser four minutes later and Jeff volleyed Albion ahead in the 36th minute – but that slender lead was all the Albion could conjure up for the awkward visit to London Road in the second leg.

And that was a game that they had to play without Jeff Astle. He finally paid the price for soldiering on with a bad knee when he broke down in training in early December, and had to submit to a cartilage operation, which put him out of commission for six weeks. He shared a hospital ward with his captain, Graham Williams, who told the local press, "Jeff Astle and I have been comparing notes on our cartilage operations. We have been like a couple of battle-scarred veterans showing the cuts; but I am one up on him. He had a measly five stitches, I had six."

Once again, Ray Crawford stood in for Jeff, and thanks to a Tony Brown hat-trick, Albion won 4-2 at Peterborough to qualify for their first Cup Final since 1954. However, in the marathon that was the League, Jeff was sorely missed, as their championship challenge faltered badly, and they went out of the FA Cup at the first attempt, at Second Division Bolton.

Of course, in those days, a cartilage operation was a serious matter. Sometimes, it could mean the end of a football career, but Jeff toiled through the winter to get fit again. It was February before he got back into the first team squad, at Hillsborough, but before that, on February 19, he had a try-out in the Central League game at home to Preston, as reported by the *Albion News.* "Jeff Astle made a welcome return to competitive football last Saturday, and obliged by scoring with almost his first kick in our Reserve game against Preston at The Hawthorns, which we won 5-0, the others being scored by Ray Crawford (2) and Ray Wilson (2). Jeff played two more games for the Stiffs, scoring at Stoke in a 4-1 defeat, but failing to register in the "mini-Derby" against the Villa.

Seven days after the Villa game, Jeff returned to first team duty – and he could not have picked a more vital game, as, on March 9, Albion travelled to the East End to face West Ham in the first leg of the League Cup Final. The Hammers had a good home record

An angry Jeff has to be restrained after scoring against Everton's Gordon West, who had been fouling him all night

against the Albion, having beaten them 4-0 in January, and, of course, 6-1 the previous season. Albion were on a poor run, having won just three of their previous ten games without Jeff, and they knew they would have to rely on resolve, and they would simply have to scrap for a result against the European Cup Winners' Cup holders.

And Jimmy Hagan had problems with team selection. Both Gerry Howshall and Bobby Hope were unfit, which let in Astle and young Graham Lovett, whilst the unlucky Stan Jones, who had played in every previous cup game, was rested for the Final, in favour of 22 year old Danny Campbell, who was making his first team team in a major Cup Final. The full team was: *Potter, Cram, Fairfax, Fraser, Campbell, Williams, Brown, Astle, Kaye, Lovett, Clark.*

West Ham were looking to complete a unique cup treble, having won the F A Cup in 1964 and the ECWC in 1965, but it was Albion who scored first, just before the break, Astle netting a glorious goal from a cross by Clive Clark. Bobby Moore equalised with a low shot and in injury time, with the Albion defenders looking for offside, 'Budgie' Byrne scored the Hammers' winner. Albion had been unlucky, for both of the West Ham goals had an element of luck, and they were confident for the home leg.

In between the two cup games, Albion turned out another couple of below par performances, drawing at Stoke and losing at home to Burnley, but the

In the limelight—Jeff looks exhausted as Graham Williams holds up the League Cup

34

game at The Hawthorns stirred the public's imagination – it was not every day that you played a Cup Final on home soil – and on a cold March evening 31,925 fans packed into the ground to roar on their favourites. For Albion there was just one change to the side that had lost at Upton Park, Bobby Hope returning in place of the injured Lovett, and with the Scot having a great game in midfield, Albion simply tore through the Londoners' defence in the first half. "Probably the finest 45 minutes of football that I ever played in," recalled Jeff later, "And my favourite night ever, at The Hawthorns."

It took just nine minutes to wipe out West Ham's aggregate lead when Cram surged forward to set up Kaye to open the scoring on the night. With the Hammers reeling, Tony Brown made it 2-0 when he bravely headed over Jim Standen's flailing fists, with Clive Clark making sure on the goal line. In the 26th minute Clark scored the third goal, with another brave, diving header, driving an already ecstatic crowd into a frenzy. The *Express and Star* described the climax of a wonderful half of attacking football; "The fourth goal after 34 minutes was a spectacular 25 yard shot from skipper Williams, that went in off a post. The way was opened by Hope with another long pass that was headed down in typical fashion by Astle."

That goal effectively clinched the cup – and a Fairs Cup place – for Albion, who merely toyed with West Ham in the second half, conceding a goal from Martin Peters to end up on the right side of a 5-3 aggregate win. It was Jeff's first major honour in the game, just seventeen months after leaving the Fourth Division, and it was with some delight that he collected his winners' tankard from Football League President Len Shipman.

Suitably inspired, Albion finished the season with a flurry, unbeaten in their last nine games, winning six and drawing three. In the process they scored 21 goals, with Jeff banging home six of them to finish the season with 18

Jeff celebrates in the dressing room after the League Cup Final win against West Ham

goals from 27 games in the League – plus another six goals from seven League Cup ties.

The now famous forward line of Brown, Astle, Kaye, Hope and Clark had rattled in 61 goals between them. All in all, the side had scored 91 League goals, and finished a creditable sixth in the table. Had it not been for Astle's mid-season injury, they may well have gone close to winning the League, as, in the end, they only finished eleven points adrift of champions Liverpool – who they took three points from during the campaign.

As a reward for winning the League Cup, the Albion directors took the team off on an exotic tour, to South America, departing a few days after the end of the domestic season. They got off to a good start, opening with a couple of wins in Lima, capital of Peru, beating first Alianza, 3-2, and then Sporto Cristal, 2-1.

It was in Lima that Astle had a rare set-to with his manager. Jeff entered the dressing room at half time to be met by an irate Hagan, who laid into his centre-forward, accusing him of shirking. In the heat of the moment, Jeff snapped, and threw his shirt at Hagan. "If you think you could do better, get out there and play yourself!" Typically, Hagan kept his cool, and pointed out that he was paid to manage – and Jeff was paid to play; "So get out there and play!"

Moving south to Rio de Janiero, Albion stopped in a hotel overlooking the twelve mile stretch of the famous Copacabana beach, where Jeff and Tony Brown played games of beach football with the talented local youngsters. The tour continued with two games in Uruguay, against international teams which were preparing for their forthcoming trip to England for the World Cup (Albion drawing 0-0 and losing 2-0 against a side that would soon hold the full England side at Wembley). Jeff was substituted in both games in Montevideo, and later admitted that he was treating the tour more as a holiday than a working trip, which added credence to Hagan's suspicions in Lima. Jeff wanted to go home!

So crowded was Albion's schedule that they had to cancel games in Mexico and Peru (against crack side Universitario De Deportes), as well as a game against River Plate, but they did play a game in Argentina, a goalless draw against Newell's Old Boys.

The last game of the tour was back in Rio, when Albion played Flamengo in the famous – but on this occasion, very empty — 200,000-capacity Maracana Stadium. They won 2-1, but once again Jeff took it easy, and ended the trip without a goal to his name. Three years later he would return to South America – although not with the Albion — and goals would be very much on the agenda.

Europe... and Q.P.R. 1966-67

There was an optimistic mood around The Hawthorns at the start of the '66-67 season. The Albion were League Cup holders, had qualified for European football for the first time, and were, without doubt, the most entertaining side in the League, with their marvellous brand of high-octane attacking football under Hagan. They even had pretensions for the championship itself – a trophy that the club had won only once, back in 1920. After all, had Jeff not been out injured for that key spell in mid-season, who knows what might have happened in the previous season. However, the club, the players and the fans were in for a rude awakening.

The opening game of the season was at Old Trafford, under a boiling, almost Mediterranean sun. In front of a fanatical United crowd of over 41,000, Albion went a goal down after just thirty seconds of the new season, scored by George Best. And it got worse.

Nobby Stiles made it two in eight minutes before Bobby Hope managed to pull a goal back, but United continued to pour forward and before 21 minutes had elapsed, they held a 5-1 lead, thanks to further goals from Herd and Denis Law (2). It looked as if there could be a record score (Albion's worst-ever defeat in the League was a 10-3 hammering at Stoke in the thirties) but United took their collective feet off the accelerator in the second half, and Clive Clark scored twice for the Albion, to make the scoreline almost respectable, at 5-3 to United. Jeff, by his own admission, hardly had a kick all game.

Four days later, Jeff got off the mark for the season, with a great shot after John Kaye had hit the crossbar, but Albion still went down 2-1 to Leeds United at Elland Road. Unfortunately, after opening their home programme when Burnley came to The Hawthorns on the Saturday, Albion were still pointless after three games, as the Clarets went away with a 2-1 win. Crisis time.

As so often happens, that bad start set the tone for the whole of the season. There was immediately a slight improvement, as the side hauled themselves off the bottom of the table by winning three of their next four games – but they then only won four out of the next sixteen.

Yet in their defense of the League Cup, Albion could do no wrong. They opened another great run in the competition at The

Hawthorns on Wednesday September 14, with a marvellous 6-1 thrashing of Aston Villa – their best win against their ancient rivals since W 'G' Richardson scored four in a 7-0 win at Villa Park in 1935. Albion were three up in 29 minutes, through Fraser (2) and Hope. In the second half, some unselfish play by Jeff helped Hope complete his hat-trick, and Clive Clark added the sixth goal.

By now, Albion's confidence, if not up to the heights of the previous season, was good enough for the side to contemplate the next trip, to Goodison Park, with some sense of expectation. And the result was one of the games of the season, in the whole Football League.

And Jeff started the football jamboree. In the seventh minute Clark swung in a high ball for Astle, lurking at the far post, and he rose above posse of defenders to head forcefully past the Everton keeper. Eight minutes later Everton equalised when Young raced onto a lob from Alan Ball to finish with a low shot that went in off the post. Three minutes after that Alan Ball mesmerised four Albion defenders before slipping a pass through to Temple, who touched the ball home as Rick Sheppard rushed off his line. Three minutes before the break, Everton were sitting pretty at 3-1, when Morrissey collected a pass from Fred Pickering to drive home into the corner.

Hagan's men went straight into the attack after the break, in an attempt to pull the game out of the fire, but any meaningful sort of comeback seemed impossible early in the second half, when Alan

Jeff gets a boot in the face for his pains — but scores against the Villa

Ball made it 4-1 to the home side. Doug Fraser replied instantly, firing a low shot under the diving West in the 50th minute. Soon after, John Kaye hit the bar, but by the 74th minute, Albion were right back in it, when Bobby Cram scored from the spot after Kaye had been brought down by Brian Labone. Two minutes later, with the huge crowd in a frenzy, Kaye headed in an inswinging free kick from Fraser – and, incredibly, it was 4-4.

Still Albion attacked; and that was their downfall, as, six minutes from the end, Everton broke away and Ian Collard was forced to bring down Alan Ball in the box. The flame-haired midfielder picked himself up, and smashed the spot-kick past Sheppard.

Nine goals – and not one from Jeff. In the last minute Jeff ran in onto a Fraser cross, and West performed miracles, first to charge down the initial shot, then to desperately clutch Jeff's follow-up – which, had it gone in, would have seen the first-ever 5-5 draw in the Albion's history.

In later years, Jeff would remember the game as the classic it surely was. "In terms of sheer entertainment, I can recall having seen few better games." Graham Williams had his own theory for the way in which Everton tore into the Baggies that night. "The lads turned out in our new all-red strip; that alone must have been an added incentive to the Everton team since anything in red must remind them of the old enemy at Anfield."

Albion's up-and-down form continued after the Goodison game, a 1-0 home defeat by Stoke City being followed by another goal feast – a 4-3 defeat against Sheffield United at Bramall Lane, with Jeff scoring the opening goal of another bonanza.

By the time the third round of the League Cup rolled round, Albion had a meagre total of just six points from ten League games – and an astonishing goals total of 23-23! The cup was a welcome relief from the struggle of the League, and newly-promoted Manchester City were beaten 4-2 at The Hawthorns – with Jeff, who had a difficult time against George Heslop – scoring Albion's second goal in the 63rd minute.

Jeff picked up an injury in the City game, and consequently missed his first game of the season, at Roker Park, on the following Saturday. That was one of several injuries that was causing Hagan concern, put his patched-up side – one of the youngest ever fielded by the Albion – did well to grab a 2-2 draw at Sunderland.

Jeff returned for the next game, against Aston Villa. He was soon back in scoring form, bravely diving in – and getting a kick in the face from Keith Bradley – to head the ball home after Dick Krzywicki's cross had hit the crossbar. The Albion eventually won that game 2-1, but things were going badly wrong at The Hawthorns. In twelve League games, Hagan had been forced to use no less than twenty players, a staggering total.

What was worse was that the simmering disquiet that had long been under the surface in the dressing room, was once again coming to the surface, just as it had during the bitter "tracksuit saga." long before Jeff's arrival. Club captain Graham Williams, who had been in and out of the side, Gerry Howshall – very much out of favour – and Stan Jones, who was still smarting over his treatment in the previous season's League Cup Final, had all demanded transfers in September, and they were soon joined by young goalkeeper Rick Sheppard, who had lost his place in the side to veteran Ray Potter. The young Bristol-born keeper was so worried about his future that he had postponed his wedding. Winger Ken Foggo was already on the list – and the next player to want away was Jeff Astle, although Hagan did not go as far as allowing the name his best striker to actually be circulated to interested clubs.

There is no question that Hagan was rubbing up his senior players the wrong way, but their main complaint was the punishing training schedule. No matter how many games they were playing – and with the League Cup and the Fairs' Cup, as well as the League, the games were coming thick and fast – Hagan's relentless training regime continued. Jeff had no doubt that it was this "over-training" that was at least partly responsible for the team's poor form; "We were burned out before we reached the field."

Two games a week was now the norm at the Albion. After a notable win at Highbury in the League, Albion travelled to the County Ground, Swindon, to continue their great run in the League Cup. It was Jeff who finally made the breakthrough in the 83rd minute of a tough game, with a typical header from a Campbell Crawford cross. Three minutes from time Jeff turned provider, when he steered a through ball for Clive Clark to seal a somewhat fortunate victory for the holders.

There may have been troubles, on and off the field, but Jeff was always the life and soul of the dressing room – and the team coach – as well as being the butt of many a joke. John Kaye recalled one incident on the way to the Swindon game. "We stopped for a meal, and were served with steak. All but Jeff, that is. While we were all chewing away, he sat with nothing in front of him, wondering when it was his turn to eat. Most of us had finished eating by the time that Jeff discovered that his steak had been grabbed by one of the non-playing members of the squad. The 'Nottingham Flash' did get a couple of small portions and had to make up with mushrooms and tomatoes."

Albion's season continued with a 2-1 defeat at home to Sheffield Wednesday – hardly the best preparation for the club's first-ever European tie. On November 2 Albion jetted to Holland to meet DOS Utrecht in the second round of the European Cities Fairs' Cup, having been awarded a bye in the first round. Jeff played in that historic tie. "We stepped onto the pitch in Holland in the coldest weather I've known. It was well below zero and the wonder was that we were able to run, let away to scheme an opening goal from Bobby Hope." That goal from the Scottish midfielder was the first of many for Albion in European football over the years, but it was not enough to grab a win, as the Dutch side equalised through van der Linden. Jeff was a little disappointed with his performance, claiming extenuating circumstances. "The lighting was the worst I'd ever played under. When the ball was crossed from the wing I would lose sight of it until the last few seconds, which was the cause of a lot of mistimed jumping."

Albion won the second leg 5-2, thanks to a Tony Brown hat-trick, but Jeff remembers the game, against the Dutch part-timers, as a real struggle. "At one stage the aggregate score was 3-3 and with away goals counting double the Dutch were ahead; but the fans roared us to our first European victory."

In November 1966, Jeff's goals dried up. He completely lost his form, and without his goals, Albion's League position began to dip once more. Cup success was all very well, but confidence was generally at a low ebb, and the relegation clouds were gathering. Jeff's solution was to ask Hagan to drop him! "When I stopped scoring, I badly needed to regain some confidence, so I asked Hagan for a run out in the Reserves. He refused. "A spell is the Reserves is not advisable for an established player." Maybe not – but by November 19, following a 2-1 defeat at Filbert Street, Jeff had been dropped, for the first time since he left Notts County, missing games against Liverpool and West Ham

When the first team travelled to Upton Park to play West Ham, Jeff was lining up for the second team at home to the Villa. He marked his Central League debut with a goal in a 5-3 win. With a goal under his belt at last, Jeff was a little more confident when he was recalled to the first team for the League Cup tie at Northampton. On his last visit to the County Ground, Jeff had hit a hat-trick in a thrilling 4-3 win. But this was not the Jeff of old, and try as he might, he could not get onto the scoresheet, although Albion did progress to the semi-final with a 3-1 win – amazingly, Jeff had still never appeared on the losing side for Albion in a League Cup tie.

The next two visitors to The Hawthorns were from Manchester – and they only helped to dig Albion's relegation hole a little deeper. First City – who had been beaten 4-2 on the same ground in the League Cup – won 3-0. Seven days later top of the table United came to town. Albion were in dire straits, in 21st position in Division One, just two points ahead of Blackpool, but they were desperate for revenge for that opening day 5-3 hammering at Old Trafford.

The game, featured on the *BBC's Match of The Day*, turned out to be another classic, even though, once again, it did not go Albion's way. It was not long before the 32,000 crowd – Albion's best of the season – got their first goal, when Aston crossed for David Herd to head past Potter in the fifth minute. Three minutes later, Jeff recorded his first ever goal on national television, when he headed home Fraser's cross, only for Herd to restore United's lead soon after. John Kaye levelled once more, only for Denis Law to put United ahead once more. In the 42nd minute Herd completed his hat-trick, only for Jeff to make it 3-4 with another bullet header from a Hope cross. Seven goals in the first half – a fantastic match. However, much as they pressed in the second half, Albion could not snatch an equaliser, although John Kaye did hit the crossbar in the dying seconds.

The Christmas fixtures summed up Albion's inconsistency. After two good results – and four much-needed points – from Tottenham, Albion were blitzed 5-1 at Turf Moor, with new signing (from Burnley) John Talbut marking his return to his former club by scoring the only League goal of his career – in the wrong net!

On January 18 Albion met up once again in the League Cup with West Ham. Having beaten them 5-3 over two legs in the 1966 Final, this time the two clubs met in the two-legged semi-finals of the same competition. This time the first leg was at The Hawthorns and, once again, Albion were in rampant form against the Irons – with Jeff leading the charge. He opened the scoring after just fifty seconds, when he outjumped Ken Brown to head home an Ian Collard cross. Fifteen minutes later Clive Clark made it 2-0, and eight minutes after that, Astle scored his second, when he latched onto a deflected shot from John Kaye to wrongfoot Standen in the West Ham goal.

On the stroke of half time, Jeff completed his hat-trick – the most important of his career – when he dribbled past two men and finished with an emphatic shot, to give Albion a 4-0 lead at the interval. And that was how it stayed. Jeff had done enough – and he certainly impressed the reporter from the *Daily Express*. "This was one of Astle's best performances. He outshone West Ham's World Cup hero Geoff Hurst, as a runner and as a striker. He scored a hat-trick and got the ball into the net twice more, only to have the goals disallowed." The victory was all the sweeter because it virtually assured Albion of a Final – but this time at Wembley. "That gave us every incentive for making sure we didn't collapse in the second leg at West Ham," recalled Jeff.

Before that second leg, there was the matter of two more cup ties. First was another trip to the County Ground, where Albion repeated their 3-1 win over Northampton, this time in the FA Cup. Once again, Jeff continued his new-found scoring form with an unstoppable shot from a Bobby Hope pass.

Then, on Wednesday February 1, in was the Fairs' Cup, and Jeff extended his football experience by playing in Italy for the first time. The tie was against powerful Serie A side Bologna, whose coach Carniglia had been impressed by Jeff's hat-trick against a West Ham side containing three of England's World Cup stars. He made sure his players paid special attention to Albion's young star, who recalled that he was snuffed out of the game. "The match was played in a vast stadium, and the 15,000 crowd looked a mere handful. The Italians had some great players and they completely outclassed us 3-0. Yugoslav Janic was very strong in the air – and never

Jeff organises the card school on the Albion team coach

43

gave me an inch."

Back in England on the Saturday, Albion broke new ground once more by appearing on the new ITV football highlights programme, *Star Soccer*, for the first time, in their game at Stoke City. Jeff scored Albion's equaliser in a 1-1 draw marred by the sending off of former Albion defender Maurice Setters, but later picked up an ankle injury which would keep him out of the second leg of the League Cup semi-final at Upton Park. No mind – a 2-2 draw ensured that it would be Albion who would face Third Division Queens Park Rangers at Wembley on March 4 1967.

Despite the poor result in Italy, Albion, for all their poor form in the League, were, at this point, still chasing three cups. That was soon to change. On Saturday February 18 they lost 5-0 to Leeds at Elland Road in the fourth round of the FA Cup – the Albion's worst result in 84 years in a competition which they had always embellished.

Worse was to come; much worse. Albion prepared for their first visit to Wembley since 1954 by taking the players away to Lilleshall for three days' training. Despite the importance of the game, Hagan would not change his training schedule, subjecting his players to the hardest routines imaginable, to the extent of arranging a full-scale practice match on the Friday before the Final.

QPR were a Third Division side – but they were a class above the rest of the sides in that division, and were running away with the title. Manager Alec Stock had assembled a side that had a good mix of youth and experience, including Jim Langley, Les Allen and the irrepressible Rodney Marsh – a side good enough to thoroughly humiliate Birmingham City over the two legs of their semi-final.

It was a game that Albion just could not afford to lose – defeat at Wembley against a Third Division side could have incalculable effects of the morale of a side already in serious trouble in the First Division. Jeff, unusually for him, was very nervous before the game; understandably so, before the biggest game of his career so far. "For the first time in my life I was plagued by nerves beforehand. Sitting in the Wembley dressing room, waiting for the bell to ring to go out on the pitch was a bit of an ordeal. It was all a bit daunting for me; being Wembley, it was almost like a state occasion. But when I got onto the pitch my nerves vanished."

Albion clicked into gear straight away. In the seventh minute Collard breached the Rangers' defence with a through ball pass to Fraser, who fed Astle and he, in turn found Clive Clark, who opened the scoring. After Springett saved a good shot from Jeff,

Albion went further ahead – again through Clark, who was enjoying himself against his former club – in the 35th minute.

Alec Stock had some task in geeing up his players for the second half. In fact, he hardly tried. "My opinion was that we were beaten. I looked for excuses and decided that we would settle for 'losing well.' I told my team that there were at least 30,000 QPR supporters in the crowd, and that they expected us to entertain them by playing football."

There have been many rumours what was said in the Albion dressing room at half time, but according to Jeff, nothing untoward was said. "Hagan just told us to keep playing our usual game. That was all. What I remember is that what it looked like in the second half was if the two sides had gone in and simply swapped shirts. There was that much of a turnaround."

On the hour Roger Morgan headed home a free kick to put Rangers back into the game. With sixteen minutes to play Rodney Marsh went on a long, languorous run that he finished with a shot that bobbled just inside the post. Jeff was taken aback. "All I could hear was the Rangers fans singing 'Rodnee, Rodnee' – I'll never forget it!"

In the 81st minute Lazarus, completed QPR's return from the dead — and broke the Albion fans' hearts — with a controversial winner. scoring after Albion's keeper Rick Sheppard had been flattened by an illegal challenge. It was a sad end to Albion's remarkable winning run in the League Cup that had looked as if it would be extended into a third season.

A grim picture in the Albion dressing room after the defeat by Third Division QPR

45

Jeff reserved his sympathy for his manager. "At the end of the game he didn't storm into the dressing room, or abuse us. His grim expression was enough. Everyone was gutted. You've seen the picture, of us in the dressing room after the game, but of all the sad hearts in the Midlands on the night of March 4 1967, Jimmy Hagan's was the heaviest."

Disastrously, four days later, the Albion players had to pick themselves up from the most humiliating experience of their careers to face mighty Bologna at The Hawthorns, in the second leg of their Fairs' Cup tie. It was no contest – with German World Cup star Helmut Haller outstanding, Albion were outclassed, going down to a 6-1 aggregate defeat, still their worst-ever defeat in Europe. "Bologna were a class above us; the best club side I have ever played against," claimed Jeff at the time.

Eliminated from all three cup competitions in the space of four weeks, at least Albion could concentrate of saving themselves from relegation. The key game in their recovery was that at Maine Road on March 25 – when it was their turn to turn around a two goal deficit. Unlike QPR, they may not have won the game, but the reward of a point from a game in which they seemed dead and buried served to revitalise the Albion's season. In the last ten games of the season, Albion won eight and drew one, including a famous 1-0 win – with Jeff scoring the goal — over Liverpool at Anfield, who helped ensure that the championship would go to Old Trafford rather than Liverpool. But Albion were not concerned with that end of the table. What mattered to them was that Albion stopped up – and Aston Villa went down.

Just a week after that win at Anfield – on May 3 1967 – Jimmy Hagan was sacked. A season which had promised so much had delivered nothing – and iron man Hagan had paid the price. There was more than a hint of sadness for Jeff as he contemplated the departure of the manager who had signed him from Notts County. "I can't help thinking that if he had relaxed just a little bit – and shown a few touches of humour when dealing with the players – he could have developed into one of England's finest managers."

Jeff finished the season with sixteen goals from 35 League games – plus another six in the cup competitions. It was a useful tally for a striker in a struggling side, and it proved that Jeff would be an important asset for the new Albion manager – whoever that was going to be...

The King and the F.A. Cup 1967-68

In May 1967, Albion appointed their new manager. Speculation had been rife that Ronnie Allen would get the job, but instead, the man chosen was Alan Ashman, a relative unknown who had worked wonders at one of football's outposts, Carlisle. Jeff certainly had little idea who he was. "I wasn't aware of Ashman's background. It wasn't until Graham Williams mentioned that he used to be centre-forward at Forest that I realised that I must have seen him play when I was a lad."

Like Jimmy Hagan, Ashman had played for Sheffield United, before leaving for Forest for five seasons, until he moved north to Brunton Park in 1951, where he scored over a hundred goals for Carlisle, in just 206 games. After finishing early as a player because of a knee problem, he coached at Penrith, whilst working at a poultry farm run by a Carlisle director, Mr Monkhouse – who offered him the manager's job in 1963.

Ashman did a great job with strictly limited resources, taking Carlisle from Division Four to within a few points of the First Division in 1967, and those achievements attracted the attention of the Albion board, who swooped to sign him.

Initially, Jeff found Ashman likable, mild-mannered and easy-going – "He didn't look or sound like your typical football manager," recalled Jeff, no doubt with Hagan's sergeant-major voice still ringing in his ears. However, when Jeff was late for one of Ashman's first training

The side that Alan Ashman was to take to the 1968 FA Cup Final

sessions, he was severely rebuked by his new boss. "If you want to play at this club, you keep to schedules – and if you buckle down, I'll make you a better player." Jeff soon began to enjoy his training under an experienced centre-forward again – "Alan concentrated on more ball practice techniques, and looked to improve your individual skills."

Ashman's first games in charge of the club were for the pre-season tour of the West Country, and the side won all three games, at Bristol City and Bournemouth, with Jeff scoring a couple of goals. In the League, things were not so rosy, as the season started badly, both for the Albion and for Jeff.

The opening game of the season , at home to Chelsea, was lost 1-0, and the side only managed to draw 3-3 at Wolves in the next game because Tony Brown punched home an injury-time equaliser. That goal so enraged Wolves keeper Phil Parkes that he ran amok, jumping on the referee's back and punching Jeff, and was sent off. Things got even worse, with a four goal drubbing at Southampton in the next game. Ashman had to act, and he dropped John Kaye and moved Jeff to centre-forward, for the first time since February 19656. He scored Albion's first goal in a 4-1 win over Wolves, and from then on, to the end of his Albion career, the number shirt belonged to Jeff.

However, the win over the Wolves was Ashman's only victory in his first half dozen games – and that was Jeff's only goal – so on September 9 Jeff was dropped to the bench for the trip to Stoke, where Graham Williams missed a penalty in a goalless draw. Worse was to come; a few days later Third Division Reading dumped Albion out of the League Cup at Elm Park – their second successive such defeat against lowly opposition in the competition.

Ashman made more changes for the next game, against his old club Nottingham Forest, and the unlikely scoring combination of Bobby Hope and Ken Stephens gave him a 2-1 win. The next game was a high profile game against First Division newcomers Coventry City at Highfield Road, a game that Jeff was keen to win. "We were anxious to make amends to Alan for our bad start, but it turned out to be one of those matches where things all went wrong."

Jeff gave Albion the lead, but Coventry stormed back to lead, through Brian Lewis and Ronnie Rees. Although Clive Clark equalised just after half time, Ernie Machin and Ronnie Rees gave the Sky Blues a 4-2 win to humiliate the Baggies. Ashman was furious, and went public with his anger in the press, shocking his players. "Coventry played with great spirit and in the competitive sense, had us licked. I never want to see Albion fold up like this again! The players got together, as Jeff remembered, "We decided to roll up our sleeves and make it up to him, with hard work and effort."

The next game was at The Hawthorns, and Sheffield United, who were one place below the Albion, in 21st position, were the visitors. The home fans, disenchanted by their poor start, stayed away, and only 15,000 turned up. They saw Jeff slam the ball into the United net after just six minutes, after Clive Clark had misdirected a header at goal. On the half hour mark Hope's precision pass sent Stephens away, and when he pulled the ball back, Astle outjumped Ken Mallender to head past Hodgkinson. Two minutes before the break Reece pulled a goal back, but Albion bounced back in the second half. In the 56th minute Bobby Hope laid a square pass into the path of Tony Brown, who fired into the net. After considerable pressure form the Albion, Jeff completed his hat-trick when he put away the loose ball after Clark's shot had rebounded off the keeper.

It seemed as if Ashman's decision to "go public" with his dissatisfaction had paid dividends. In their next fourteen games, Albion lost just three times. The run included wins against Leeds (2-0), Burnley (8-1 – Albion's biggest win since beating Manchester City 9-2 in 1957), Spurs (2-0) and back-to-back away wins at West Ham (3-2) and Chelsea (3-0). The run culminated with their best League performances of the season over Christmas. On Boxing Day Albion, in eighth spot, entertained third place Manchester City, and the result was a real thriller. Albion took a two goal half time lead, one from Tony Brown, the other a trademark header from Jeff, from Bobby Hope's corner kick. In the second half City completely outplayed the Baggies, and Francis Lee and Mike Summerbee scored to level matters, and Graham Williams made a remarkable goal line clearance to prevent a City winner. Just when City thought they had earned a point. Jeff struck again, Tony Brown slipping the ball to him for an 89th minute winner. Four days later Albion won 2-0 at Maine Road to complete a noteworthy "double" against the side that were to win the championship that season.

Albion had undergone a remarkable transformation since the embarrassment of Highfield Road. Now they were in fifth place, just eight points behind leaders Manchester United, and Jeff had already recorded fourteen goals in the League. Jeff had his own views on who was responsible for the improvement. "There is no doubt that once we pulled ourselves together, Ashman exuded an air of calmness and understanding, and the club was happier than it had been for years."

Ashman was modesty personified. He insisted that the Albion's success was purely down to the players. "There was plenty of talent at the club when I arrived. I merely gave them confidence in themselves and offered them the chance to justify the faith everybody at the club had in them." Unfortunately, as far as their title credentials were concerned, the bubble burst somewhat just as the FA Cup third round came round, as they lost 4-1 to fellow title contenders Liverpool, and 3-2 at Nottingham Forest.

The third round of the Cup was a respite from those two poor performances in the League, but it also held its dangers. They had twice been eliminated from the League Cup by smaller clubs, and their trip to Fourth Division Colchester on Saturday January 27 had all the makings of an upset.

The small Essex garrison town had been infected by a strong dose of Cup fever. They had not seen a First Division club at Layer Road since Arsenal went there in 1959, and the game was a sell-out. Their manager, Neil Franklin, had watched Albion's two defeats at Liverpool and Nottingham, and thought he had some idea of Albion's weak spots.

The First Division side started nervously as Colchester tore into them. The Albion defence was looking anything but happy, and it was no surprise when United took the lead in the eighth minute. Martin put over a dangerous cross and when Osborne missed his punch, Reg Stratton headed into an empty net.

There were several more scares for the Baggies before they equalised in the 38th minute, Tony Brown converting a penalty after Duncan Forbes had fouled Jeff in the area.

That goal settled the Albion's jitters. In the second half they were calmer and far more controlled in their play, and managed to restrict Colchester's attacking ambitions to a few isolated breaks. Eight minutes form the end Franklin threw on Mickey Bullock for McKechnnie for one last attempt to win the game. In the last minute Stratton glanced a header against the bar and the substitute put away the rebound. The crowd went wild and John Talbut picked the ball out of the net and kicked it over the stand – "That's us finished with the Cup for another year!"

Astonishingly, referee Jones (who had, coincidentally, officiated at Jeff's Albion debut at Leicester) disallowed the goal, for handball against Bullock. It was an offence which only he saw – but it helped Albion win the Cup! Jeff certainly missed the foul; "We came off the pitch with nobody having any idea why the referee disallowed the goal."

For the replay the following Wednesday, Albion would make no further mistakes. An astonishing gate of over 40,000 turned up at The Hawthorns to see their side win 4-0, with Jeff recording his first two cup goals of the season.

Things did not improve in the League, with a 1-0 home defeat against Coventry, followed by a 1-1 draw against Sheffield United, 17-year old debutant Asa Hartford setting up a goal for Jeff at Bramall Lane. In the fourth round of the Cup Albion were drawn at home to Southampton, who could field Jimmy Gabriel, a Cup winner with Everton in 1966, Frank Saul, who had scored Spurs' winner in the 1967 Final, and Ron Davies – one of the few players who could genuinely rival Jeff as a header of a ball.

It was Davies, in fact, who helped the Saints to a 1-0 half time lead, heading on for Saul to beat Osborne. Albion equalised with a freak goal from Tony Brown, the ball hitting a divot to deceive the Southampton keeper, but as Jeff recalled, they knew that the replay at the Dell – where they had already lost 4-0 – would be a tough one. "It was a very wet night, very heavy conditions and Southampton are a strong side, and very physical. We expected a difficult game, and got one."

It was an epic encounter, and in keeping with Albion's long tradition in the FA Cup. Southampton took a tenth minute lead through Saul, who put the ball away just as Osborne dived at his feet. The Albion keeper was concussed, but resumed after lengthy treatment, with trainer Stuart Williams camped behind his goal to keep a watchful eye.

Astle equalised for Albion in the 16th minute, when he slammed home a John Kaye pass, and by the break Albion were ahead, thanks to Tony Brown, who scored after Gabriel had gifted him the ball. During the half time interval the club doctor examined Osborne and advised him not to go out for the second half. Graham Williams took over in goal, Lovett came on as substitute and John Kaye dropped back into defence. Jeff was injured soon after, in a hefty collision, and was carried off, only to return after a few minutes, but while he was off Fisher scored

Jeff scores the Albion's injury time winner in a great cup-tie at Southampton

Southampton's equaliser against the ten men. With the game at fever pitch, and heading for another gruelling thirty minutes, Lovett hit a shot against the woodwork and a limping Astle rapped the ball home. Surprisingly, the home side had failed to really trouble Williams in goal – he spent more time dodging missiles thrown by the Saints fans, including a sock filled with nuts and bolts!

Jeff had another storming game in the fifth round tie at Second Division Portsmouth, where he kept up his goal a game record with a 30th minute header from a Bobby Hope free kick. Five minutes later, Clive Clark scored a second, and although Hiron pulled a goal back in the 73rd minute, the result was never really in doubt. After the match an unimpressed Portsmouth manager, George Smith declared, "If West Brom win the Cup, I will eat my hat!"

Back in the League, Albion had two successive home games. In the first they beat Stoke 3-0, and Jeff, in the absence of Tony Brown, scored his first-ever penalty. Three days later, Everton – who were also still in the Cup – arrived at West Bromwich, and won 6-2. Alan Ball had a great game, and scored four times, as Albion left the field to jeers from their own fans. Everton left with both points – and their fans left with the sugar. Tate and Lyle were on strike in Liverpool, so the Toffees supporters raided all the supermarkets in West Bromwich and stripped the shelves of all the sugar they could find. Sweet success indeed…

The next visitors to The Hawthorns also hailed from Merseyside, as Albion were drawn against Liverpool in the quarter finals of the Cup. In each of the three previous rounds Liverpool had stonewalled for a goalless draw (at Bournemouth, Walsall and Tottenham) and won the replay at Anfield. They repeated the first part of that recipe, although, in truth, they should have won at the first time of asking, as Geoff Strong hit the bar, and Alf Arrowsmith missed two sitters. Jeff, marked out of the game, and missing the injured Bobby Hope, hardly had a kick.

Jeff had a nasty shock in the post a couple of days later. "I opened two letters, and both threatened injury to my wife and baby daughter should I play in the replay at Anfield. I didn't know what to do, but I realised that the best thing to do was to ignore them. I ripped them up, and never told Laraine anything."

Albion played two more goalless draws in the League, against Sunderland and Burnley, before facing Liverpool again, at Anfield. Over 54,000 people crammed into Anfield for the replay, and it was Liverpool who took the lead through Jeff's former team mate Tony Hateley, in the 25th minute. In the second half Albion attacked the Kop end and strung together a series of passing movements which set Liverpool back on their heels. In the 70th minute they equalised, as described in the

Daily Mirror. "It was Fraser's cross which really set up Astle's equaliser. It was his 24th goal of the season, and perhaps his best – the header of a conquistador – spectacular, dramatic, yet coolly judged. Astle truly silenced the Kop. Albion remained the stronger side during extra time, but the score remained 1-1 after 120 minutes.

By now, of course, the semi-final draw had been made, and Albion knew that to earn a tie against Second Division Birmingham City at Villa Park, they would have to beat Liverpool in the second replay at Maine Road on Thursday April 18. First, though, they were scheduled to play three League games in the space of four days, which was hardly the best preparation for such a titanic meeting. On Good Friday they drew 2-2 at Newcastle. The following day they played Sheffield Wednesday at home. Jeff scored Albion's goal in a 1-1 draw, but it was an incident with Wednesday centre-half Vic Mobley that attracted the headlines.

"Vic was all over me throughout the game. All the time he was pulling at my shirt. I gave him a warning. 'Do that again and you're for it.' Next ball, we went up, and in anger I put my elbow in. It was awful. I actually heard the blood gurgling out. As soon as I'd done it, I regretted it. There was a huge patch of blood which gradually spread out over his white shirt. I should have been sent off, really, but nothing happened. We shook hands afterwards, and Vic said 'Forget it' – there were never any hard feelings."

On Easter Monday, Tony Brown scored the two goals which saw off Newcastle – it was time for another crack at the Anfield giants!

In a bold move, Ashman decided to drop John Kaye back into defence to cover for the injured Eddie Colquhoun for the game at Maine Road – he also had Bobby Hope fit again. In preparation for the game Albion went training at Southport, where Jimmy Hagan had taken the side for a break during the previous season's relegation scare. The sea air worked wonders for the players, but the journey to Manchester proved a nightmare, as the coach became mired in traffic, and needed a police escort to reach the ground barely thirty minutes before the kick-off.

The rush did not seem to affect the side, any more than the huge, mostly Liverpudlian crowd of over 56,000. They took a seventh minute lead, and once again it was that man Astle, who sprinted onto a Collard through ball to surprise Lawrence on his near post.

Three minutes later, as Albion faced a red tide, Kaye and Talbut collided, and Kaye had to leave the field for several minutes, returning with his head heavily bandaged, and still bleeding. It didn't stop the tough Yorkshireman heading the ball…

Seven minutes before half time the incessant Liverpool pressure paid off when Tony Hateley headed home Ian Callaghan's centre. Early in the second half Osborne had to be alert to save two efforts from Roger Hunt, but gradually Albion began to play the better football, and they regained the lead in the 63rd minute. Substitute Kenny Stephens sent in a neat low cross, Brown flicked the ball on, and with the Liverpool defence appealing for offside, Clive Clark stroked the ball home, for what proved to be the winner. After the game, Bill Shankly ungraciously summed it up; "Our goalkeeper was a spectator, yet we lost." Jeff saw the win as a victory for attacking football. "I'm glad we won for Wembley's sake. When we went to Wembley to watch the League Cup Final between Leeds and Arsenal this season, I was so bored at half time that I went out and sat on the coach. Defensive football gets on my nerves."

Two days later an exhausted Albion went to Elland Road without Jeff, who missed his first game of the season as Albion went down 3-1. In the days leading up to the FA Cup semi-final against Birmingham City, football fever gripped the imagination of the West Midlands. There was much talk of the 1931 Cup Final, when Albion beat Blues 2-1 at Wembley, when Albion had been in the Second Division and Blues in the First. This time Birmingham were the underdogs, although they had beaten both Arsenal; and Chelsea on the way to Villa Park, and they could boast in their side

Jeff's former County team mate Ron Wylie, Barry Bridges, Trevor Hockey and ex-England centre forward Fred Pickering. The latter was desperate to reach Wembley, for in 1966 he had played in every game of Everton's run to the Final, only to be dropped for the last hurdle, against Sheffield Wednesday.

Albion, of course, had their own stars, but there was one

Left: the ball's in the net against Blues... right: Tony and Jeff celebrate in the dressing room

54

man above all that Birmingham feared. In the dressing room before the semi-final, local lad Johnny Vincent warned his Blues team mates that they would have to get at least one goal because "There is no way we will stop Astle scoring." How right he was...

Vincent, watching from the subs bench, along with 60,000 other interested parties, saw his prediction come true as early as the 13th minute. Winston Foster was penalised for a high challenge on Astle, and when Tony Brown tapped the ball to Hope, Herriott tipped his shot away, only for Astle to run on to fire home the rebound.

Albion held that lead comfortably to the interval. The second half resumed in light drizzle, and Pickering commenced a one-man assault on the Albion goal. Yet it was Albion who scored again, in the 67th minute, Hope setting up the goal with a well-timed through ball for Tony Brown. Twice more Pickering went close, heaving a goal bound shot cleared off the line by Talbut, and heading another great chance straight at Osborne, but when the final whistle went, it was the Baggies, not the Blues, who were at Wembley.

Jeff was too much of a professional not to spot the work of another centre-forward, "The best player on the pitch was Fred Pickering – but I'm sure the better team won."

Albion could now look towards their second successive appearance at Wembley – but there were still matters to see to in the League. Just two days after the semi-final, Albion played host to European Cup Finalists Manchester United, who had just eliminated real Madrid, and who were looking for a win at The Hawthorns to maintain a two point lead at the top of the First Division.

Jeff had his targets as well; he was looking to break the thirty goal barrier for the first time ever. It didn't take him long. In the ninth minute Tony Dunne put the ball right to his feet; he held off a challenge from Denis Law and struck the ball high into the net.

By the break a goal from Ronnie Rees meant Albion were two goals ahead, and soon after the turn-around, a Tony Brown penalty made it three. In the 59th minute Astle headed his 30th goal of the season from a Hope free kick, as

Jeff checks his winner's medal

Albion swamped the United defence. Law pulled a goal back from the spot, only for Asa Hartford to score the first goal of his career – from Jeff's header – to make it 5-1. Two minutes later Jeff completed an unforgettable hat-trick, when he stooped low to head in a Lovett cross. No matter that Brian Kidd scored two late goals to make the score 6-3 – it was still United's worst defeat since December 1963. United had their own 'King" on the pitch, in Denis Law, but he had been overshadowed by West Bromwich royalty that night.

Two days later, Jeff did it again, scoring another hat-trick, against his favourite opposition, West Ham, in a 3-2 win at The Hawthorns. He failed to score in the last two League games of the season, at Sunderland and Arsenal, but his final tally of 26 goals in 41 League games was his best yet in an Albion shirt.

Now all attention turned to the Final. Everton had beaten favourites Leeds in the other semi-final with a penalty from Johnny Morrissey, they had already beaten Albion twice in the League, and were the darlings of the national press. Albion went away to their lucky training headquarters at Southport to prepare. Jeff sent a final message from the Albion HQ. "It is a great feeling to be Wembley-bound, but it is something I would never even dreamed about when I left school ten years ago, as a fifteen year old. The cup run has some vivid memories for me, and I rate my goal at Anfield the best of the eight I have scored in the Cup so far. This is a good time to thank the people who have helped me in my career. My parents, Mr Sprittlehouse, head of my junior school. Then, of course, Tommy Lawton, who taught me to head a ball, Jimmy Hagan, who brought me into the First Division, and Alan Ashman, who has been such a great influence on me this

The goal that booked Jeff his place in football folklore — the Cup Final winner against Everton

season. Finally, the Albion fans. The Hawthorns crowd has been great to me; having the fans on my side has really helped me."

On Saturday May 18, it rained right up to the kick-off. The downpour ceased just as the teams reached the field to the deafening roars of the 100,000 crowd. Everton kicked off. The opening minutes were littered with fouls from both sides. Most notable was a crude challenge by Kaye on Ball, which led to referee Leo Callaghan giving the Albion man a warning. Another foul by Kaye on Harvey left the Everton fans chanting "We want football" and it was not until right on half time that Morrissey forced Osborne into the first save of the game.

In the second half Jeff went close for the Albion with a header which passed inches wide of the post. Albion were stifling the Everton midfield trio of Ball, Kendall and Harvey, but in doing so were restricting their own attacking forays, and the result was a terrible game for the purist. Right at the death Husband headed over the bar with only Osborne to beat. It was the easiest chance of the game, and it meant that extra time would have to be played at the end of a sometimes stultifying goalless draw.

For Albion, Dennis Clarke became the first substitute ever to play in an FA Cup Final, when he took over from the injured John Kaye for the last thirty minutes at a now sunny Wembley.

In the 92nd minute Doug Fraser fed Astle, who turned and swayed through the midfield. From 25 yards he shot. The ball struck Brian Labone and rebounded back to Jeff, who swung his left boot to hit a first time shot high and wide of Gordon West, to the left hand corner. Jeff had his own view of that epic goal. "I had a crack at goal, but it was not a very good shot. I had a bit of luck when the ball bounced back to me, but this time I could see all of the goal, and I hit it on the volley with my gammy left foot. To me, though, it was just as if God had said on Friday night 'The Final will end 1-0 and Jeff Astle will score the goal.' My name was on it." Fate had decreed that Jeff had scored in every round, and Albion had won the FA Cup for the first time since 1954.

Try as they might, Everton could not muster a response, as Albion, at last, dominated the game. Indeed, shortly before the final whistle, Tony Brown and Graham Lovett broke clear with just West to beat. In the end, a nervous Lovett shot wastefully over the bar,

Gordon West can only watch as the goal goes in...

but afterwards the player would later joke with Jeff, "I deliberately put it over to waste time. Otherwise it would never have been known as 'The Astle Final!'"

After a winners' banquet on the Saturday night, the team returned to West Bromwich to a heroes' welcome the following morning. Jeff had been up all night celebrating. He and Laraine, and Tony Brown and his wife Irene had talked the night away with commentator Kenneth Wolstenholme, who had earlier described Jeff's goal to the nation on *BBC TV*.

In West Bromwich, on a bright Sunday morning, over 150,000 people lined the streets. As Albion drove through on an open-top bus, the fans were everywhere; on the roof of High Street banks, on bus stops and up lamp-posts, all in an effort to see their triumphant team. The hit song *Congratulations* was played over loudspeakers as the bus neared the town hall, and when it arrived, captain Graham Williams climbed the steps to the balcony with the FA Cup. He was followed by each of the players in turn, but the biggest cheers were reserved for the heroic John Kaye – and goalscorer supreme Jeff Astle.

Back in the Black Country, it had been party time everywhere in pubs, clubs, restaurants – and even hospitals and old people's homes. In the early hours of Sunday morning, one 19 year old resident of Netherton, Kenny Norton, with his mate Harry Yardley, both of them a little worse for wear after toasting Albion's win, daubed graffiti on the Primrose Bridge, Cradley Road. Norton made his 'statement' for three reasons — he wanted to celebrate Albion's historic win and he wanted Jeff to see it every time he visited Cradley Heath Greyhound Stadium. Most important, he wanted to make sure that the people of the Black Country would always remember Jeff. The inscription he painted on the bridge was clear and simple, for all the world to see; it read "Astle is The King."

The "Astle Bridge" in Netherton—as it was later modified, in 2002

Football riots 1968-69

May 1968. Jeff had the world at his feet. He had just scored the only goal in Final of the greatest club competition in the world, becoming, at the same time, only the fifth player in history to score in every round of the FA Cup. He was the top scorer in the First Division, and surely a place in the England team was only just around the corner. But he didn't have much time to wallow in the post-Final publicity scramble; on the Tuesday the Albion team was flown out to East Africa to honour a promise to tour there to help promote British exports to the region. "I always regretted that. We just had no time to enjoy all the fuss after the Final, because in no time we were in Kenya. And when we got back the new season was upon us, and it had all been forgotten, in a way."

Albion's first game was against a Dar-es-Salaam Select XI in Tanzania, on the Thursday, and Albion, without Kaye and Osborne, both injured in the Final, were lucky to escape with a 1-1 draw, with Jeff heading a classic equaliser in the 69th minute.

Two days later Albion played the Tanzanian national side on the same ground, and drew 1-1 once more, Jeff again obliging with the goal. John Osborne was back between the posts – because Rick Sheppard had seriously burned himself under the hot equatorial sun — so badly that he could hardly bear to put on his shirt. The game got rather rough in its latter stages – a sign of what was to come on the tour.

On May 29 Albion flew to Kampala, where they were due to play the Ugandan national side at the Nakivubo Stadium. Albion won the game 1-0, despite having Graham Williams sent off, but the game was a bad one, as the *Daily Nation* reported. "This was a disgraceful match. Referee Bulenya's vacillating and anti-West Brom decisions provoked rather than curbed the visibly increasing rough house incidents that seemed to get worse with every minute."

"It was shocking," said Alan Ashman. "The referee did not seem to know the meaning of fairness. It appears that the standard of refereeing in this part of the world is not very high."

On June 1 Albion met the Kenyan national side in Nairobi, in a game to celebrate the country's Self-Government Day, with Kenya's Milton Obote and Zambia's Kenneth Kaunda the honoured guests, but it took two penalties in the last five minutes from Tony Brown, to win the game 2-1.

At the weekend the Albion party played "tourist" when they made a visit to the Tsavo National Park in Kenya, where Jeff recalled "hard man" Percy Freeman swimming across a crocodile-infested creek. Then it was back to Uganda for a second game at the Nakivubo Stadium in Kampala, scene of so much unpleasantness just seven days before. This time, instead of the national side, the locals tried an experiment; for the first time ever, the neighbouring countries of Kenya, Uganda and Tanzania had put together a joint side, managed for this match only, by the West German coach of Uganda, Burkhart Pape; there were five players in the starting line-up who had taken part in the previous brawl the week before. Watching the game were the presidents Obote, Nyere and Kaunda. Perhaps unwisely, Ashman selected both the volatile Rees and Hartford. Putting Albion's injury problems on the tour into perspective, Juma missed the game for the locals because he was suffering from malaria, which was (and is) endemic in the area.

In a tense atmosphere, in front of a packed house, the game got off to a cracking start. In the second minute Ugandan keeper Massajage made a great save from Astle, for he had no chance a minute later when Tony Brown supplied Jeff to open the scoring with a fine shot. Albion were ahead for just three minutes; tiny left winger Aziz, who had had a good game against the Albion for Tanzania, beat two defenders and crossed into the box, where Dennis Clarke handled the ball. Okech scored from the penalty spot.

Albion forced four corners, and were unlucky not to add to their score, but the game changes dramatically in the 15th minute, when Okee took out Clive Clark with a really shocking tackle. The winger was carried off, and replaced by Lovett; that tackle, effectively, ended Clark's Albion career. Three minutes later, after a classic piece of retaliation for the assault on his close friend Clark, Astle was warned by the referee, and Asa Hartford was booked, both for fouls on Okee. Still the roughness continued, and Kaye and Talbut were also warned by referee Ngaah.

At half time Alan Ashman walked into the dressing room to talk to the team. "I'd call it off here and now but there are some people in that crowd giving us some great support and if we packed it in, we'd be letting them down. We are not going to be intimidated or forced to throw in the towel. We are professionals and we are going to see this out in a professional way. I can use substitutes in the second half, but I have no intention of doing so. The team which goes out now will finish the game and we will not come off losing."

In the 57th minute the "home" side had a goal disallowed for

60

offside, but five minutes later they took the lead with a genuine goal, when Sheppard slipped and substitute Ouma took advantage of the mix-up to nip in and score.

Brown, Rees, Astle and Kaye were all subject to the most appalling body checks as the home defenders did just as they wished. Fifteen minutes from time, Hartford was sandwiched by two defenders, and exacted his own retribution, and was promptly sent off. Three minutes later, Stephen Baraza ran at Ian Collard and viciously kicked out at his right shin, putting him out of the game, and was deservedly sent off as well. The tackle – a real shocker – sparked a riot. Asa Hartford ran onto the pitch to lay into the African players for a second time, joined by several other players, as the crowd spilled onto the pitch and armed police had to run on to restore order. Graham Williams could be heard shooting to his manager, "It's hopeless, it's as bad as last time, we'll be lucky to get away alive if we don't come off now" and at one point it looked as if the captain would bring his players off, until Ashman insisted that the match continue, shouting, "Get on with it. Two teams can play this kind of stuff."

Six minutes from time Ronnie Rees pulled down a high ball down the left wing, and shot in one movement, to score a brilliant goal from 25 yards to level the scores. Amazingly, there were FOURTEEN minutes of injury time added on because of the riot and frequent stoppages. Not one Albion player escaped without some injury or other.

Jeff faces the press after the "Battle of Kampala"

The normally quiet spoken Ashman was interviewed by the *Daily Nation* after the game. "Both games in Uganda have been brawls. An absolute disgrace. We have been subjected to really nasty, vicious fouls, and in one incident in the second game Ian Collard was put out of the game by an over the top tackle of the worst kind. Then there was a riot with all of the players involved in a skirmish when Hartford got himself sent off. All of my players wanted to leave the field – not because they were scared, but because they just not want to get involved in such a match. I insisted that they remain on the field to the end, but I also told them that if it was necessary to defend themselves then they must do so. In the circumstances, the lads have behaved extremely well. The East African side got too excited; they got completely carried away." The tour ended on June 8, with a 4-3 win against Kenya in the much calmer atmosphere of Nairobi.

Back in England, Albion could not repeat their League form of the previous season, when they had qualified for the Fairs' Cup by virtue of the League placing – but were playing in the European Cup Winners' Cup because of their FA Cup win. The problem was the defence, which was leaking goals all over the place. The domestic season started in alarming fashion, with a 6-1 defeat at Maine Road, in the Charity Shield game against champions Manchester City, and there would be other similar thrashings; 4-2 at Coventry, 4-1 at Ipswich, 4-0 at Everton and West Ham, 5-1 at Maine Road in the League, and 5-2 at home to Nottingham Forest.

The attack, though, with Jeff in peak form, was as devastating as ever. He did not match his overall tally of 35 goals in the previous season, but 26 goals – 21 in the League — was still an excellent return.

And talking of returns, Jeff made an unexpected and nostalgic trip to his old hunting ground – Meadow Lane – early in the season, when Albion were drawn away to Nottingham Forest in the League Cup. After the draw had been made, Forest's Main Stand dramatically burned down, during their League game against Leeds, and the cup-tie with the Albion was switched to the Notts County ground. Albion won 3-2 and Jeff put on a fine display for family and friends by scoring twice. It would be the only time that he ever played at Meadow Lane after leaving County.

Jeff also scored two goals in another thrilling home win against European champions Manchester United, and two more in a dramatic 3-2 win at Newcastle – a real pressure match. The game was the one after the 5-2 home defeat by Forest, and Albion chairman Jim Gaunt had, rather incautiously, come out in the press insisting that Albion would win at St James' Park, to make up for the Forest drubbing.

For all their inconsistency in the League – after an in-and-out season, they ended the campaign with a seven match unbeaten run that included six goals from Jeff, and took them up to a final position of tenth in the table – the 1968-69 season will always be remembered for the club's exploits in two cup competitions.

Back in Europe, in the European Cup Winners' Cup, Albion got a tough opening draw, with a first leg game away to Belgian Cup winners Bruges. They had been watching the Albion before the game, and had clearly decided that if they could stop Jeff Astle, they would stop the Albion. And they came close to succeeding. Jeff had to put up with some treatment throughout the game, and it affected his game, Albion going down 3-1 despite a goal from 17 year-old newcomer Asa Hartford, who became the youngest-ever player to score a goal in European competition.

Jeff recalled afterwards that the match – referred to in the press for ever more as 'The Battle of Bruges' – may well have been started by the visitors. "That was Doug Fraser's fault, that was! It was typical Dougie Fraser — he went around clogging everybody, and I ended up getting kicked! It was a battle — it was a very, very tough match that was. I was in hospital that night, after the first leg, and I remember coming back on the 'plane, and I remember that out of a squad of fifteen, there were four or five of us with our shoes off, because we'd got bandages on our legs from the match the night before."

The match exploded fifteen minutes from time when Jeff clashed with the veteran Belgian international keeper, Frederick Boone — who just went berserk. Astle emerged from a scrum holding his head and was carried off unconscious on a stretcher, and taken straight to hospital. Immediately after the clash a mass of players

Jeff gets it in the neck again against Bruges

got involved in a fight, scores of fans ran on to the pitch and a couple of dozen armed police ran on; Asa Hartford had to receive treatment for a kick in the stomach and Tony Brown was chased by spectators.

Albion's task for the second leg – they now had to win 2-0 to go through on away goals – could have been even tougher, for Lambert put the ball into the Albion net just a second after the referee had blown the final whistle.

Astle was later released from hospital in Ostend, and returned to the hotel to fly home in the early hours of the morning. He had concussion, heavy bruising on the right side of his temple, and an ankle injury, the latter the result of the constant battering he had received all game, unprotected by Danish referee Mr de Haser. Not surprisingly, Jeff missed the next game, a home goalless draw with the Wolves.

The return game was always going to be unpleasant. Not surprisingly, the atmosphere was hostile in the extreme; from the start the visitors were jeered by the Hawthorns crowd who were aware of what had happened in Belgium. And the Albion defenders were happy to get their retaliation in first this time; in the first few minutes there were two Belgians writhing on the ground in agony whilst the referee played on. And three times in the first ten minutes Astle was blatantly pushed flat on the turf when he tried to reach high crosses, and again the referee took no action.

It was all Albion, though, and in the 14th minute, in the first decent bit of football, Astle managed to get away from his markers to nod down a Hartford cross for Tony Brown to crack the ball home.

Goalkeeper Boone picked up a number of pennies (large, heavy, pre-decimal!) and handed them to the referee; a warning announcement was made to the crowd, and the number of police increased. Almost immediately Boone went down in a goalmouth clash and Graham Williams used the opportunity to appeal to the Birmingham Road End to stop throwing coins.

A minute before the break Albion took an aggregate lead; Astle was sent flying, as usual, but Albion continued the move and Asa Hartford forced home the ball, to give Albion the lead on away goals.

The animosity continued in the second half, when Van den Daele was floored by a kick from Hartford which would have seen an instant dismissal in the League, but he got away without punishment; he was later withdrawn by Ashman, in favour of Collard. It was not until the last quarter of an hour that the game really hotted up again, when, as the *Daily Mail* claimed, "Some players looked as if they would be happy to continue without a ball. In fact, many incidents occurred after play had left the point of explosion." Osborne was viciously kicked on the hand long after he had cleared the ball, and Rees was twice cynically hacked down, as some of the Belgian defenders seemed to complete lose all self-control. It was a bad night for European football – but it saw Albion through to a second round tie against Dinamo Bucharest.

Incredibly, there were more riotous scenes in the Rumanian capital, as Albion fought out a 1-1 draw with ten men, after Ronnie Rees had been sent off for retaliation. Fifteen minutes from time, after a series of cynical fouls on him, Rees retaliated against Stefan, who went down as if pole-axed, writhing on the floor, resulting in the Albion winger being sent off. There was doubt about the decision; Rees had run fully 25 yards to get his own back on the Rumanian. As Rees walked off the pitch, Ashman and the five Albion substitutes were all pelted with missiles – rubble from the partially completed stadium — so that they had to leave their seats and seek safety on the touchline. Graham Williams, one of the subs, said later, "We had to run for our lives. It would have been dangerous to have stayed because the bottles and bricks were landing too close. Even when we moved we were still within range; it was unpleasant to the end."

In the last minute, Nunweiller netted for Dinamo, but was offside, and the Albion players left the field under a barrage of missiles, escorted by the home players – who put their arms around the Albion players' shoulders to protect them — to the dressing rooms. Police moved in waving batons and fighting fans brawled either side of –

Trouble in Africa, violence in Bruges; now it's a stoning in Bucharest...

and on top of – the players tunnel. Jeff later recalled, "It was terrifying. We were scared to go into the tunnel. I have never seen such a hostile mob at home or abroad."

Albion saw off Dinamo – the state-sponsored team of the Rumanian Ministry of the Interior – by four clear goals in the second leg at The Hawthorns. In the 72nd minute of that game, Jeff – who had had a seven week-long barren spell in the League – scored what would be his only goal in European competition when he converted a cross from Clive Clark, only recalled because Rees was serving an automatic one match ban for his dismissal in the first leg.

In the draw for the quarter-finals in Geneva that weekend, Albion were fortunate, in that they avoided Cologne, Torino and Slovan Bratislava – and were drawn against Scottish Cup holders Dunfermline, instantly becoming firm favourites to progress to the last four.

It was not to be, despite a gritty goalless draw in the first leg at East End Park. Only twice before, in a long series of European ties between English and Scottish clubs, had the side from north of the border progressed; and that pattern should have been maintained, as Albion dominated a second leg played at The Hawthorns in temperatures well below zero. With a biting north wind, it was so cold that kitman Dave Matthews was sent out before the game to buy gloves for all the Albion players, and visibility during the game was restricted by the huge amount of sand blown up by the wind; it had been laid down by the ton to try to soften the rock-hard pitch.

Albion controlled the game, but the Scots scored a shock goal in the second minute, and kicked everything that moved thereafter. Jeff had his moments, but the truth was, he was going through one of those spells that all top strikers have. He was way off-form, without a goal in the League for fifteen weeks, and with only young Dennis Martin alongside him, and to Bobby Hope in midfield, Albion could not score the two goals that they would have needed to overtake Dunfermline's away goal.

Jeff was concerned enough about his form to request a rare game in the Reserves when the first team's game at home to

Beaten to the ball by Peter Shilton in the Hillsborough semi-final

Ipswich fell victim to the weather, on February 22. He played – and scored – for the second team at Bolton, only for the game to be abandoned at half time.

It the Dunfermline exit was disappointing, there was worse to come. Albion had started their defence of the FA Cup, with some excellent victories, starting with a 3-0 home win over Second Division Norwich City, notable for an Astle rarity – a penalty, given to Jeff because Tony Brown, the usual penalty taker, was out injured. It got him off the mark in the Cup, but was not to be the start of another 'goal-a-round' run. Wins at Fulham, and at home to Arsenal, followed. In the sixth round, Albion won an explosive game against Chelsea at Stamford Bridge, when Jeff had a perfectly good headed goal disallowed – because referee Jim Finney awarded Albion a penalty! "I thought it was a perfectly good goal," said Jeff afterwards. "Harris tried to stop the ball with his hands, but failed."

Tony Brown took the penalty, but Bonetti made a fantastic save to push the ball around the post. No mind – eight minutes later Jeff scored what proved to be the winning goal. The game ended with a free-for-all in the Albion goalmouth, with Chelsea players kicking away at poor John Osborne, who had sat on the ball to prevent a late Chelsea equaliser.

That gave Albion a semi-final against relegation-threatened Leicester City, who had struggled to beat little Mansfield in their quarter-final If Jeff was quietly confident that Albion would beat Leicester – and why not, for it was that confidence that had regularly taken him to the top of the scoring charts – then at least one of his colleagues was perhaps over-confident. Graham Lovett put a deposit down on a new sports car, on the strength of the expected

The disappointment shows; Jeff (left) congratulates the victorious Leicester men

return to Wembley – and had to cancel the order on the Monday after the defeat to Leicester.

For that's what happened, after a sorry Albion performance at Hillsborough, where, as Jeff remembered, they went down to a late, late goal. "Allan Clarke barely touched the ball that game. He had just one kick, and it bounced thirty times before it hit the net. I just couldn't believe that we lost that game — and just four minutes from the end. Especially when I thought how well we had done to get there this time round, beating Fulham, Chelsea and Arsenal – really tough games. We had done much better this time round getting to the semi-final than we had done the year before when we won the Cup, and then we had to go out to a team like Leicester City, who were bottom of the First Division, and who were relegated at the end of the season, after losing to Manchester City in the Cup Final. We all thought it was going to be a "repeat Cup Final" – us against Everton (who lost their semi-final to Manchester City) at Wembley again, twelve months on."

So ended a disappointing season for Albion. So near, and so far. Jeff, at least, ended the season in a high note, with a return to form, a run of goals, and selection for England. With the World Cup coming up in Mexico, the 69-70 season would be a vital one for him.

The Albion line-up at the start of the 1968-69 season. Back row (l-r), Alan Merrick, Bobby Hope, Jeff Astle, Tony Brown, Dick Krzywicki, Rick Sheppard, John Talbut. Front row: Ronnie Rees, Doug Fraser, John Kaye, Graham Williams, Asa Hartford

Heading for Mexico, 1969-70

Because of his excursions with England – Jeff had been called up for the national side for their summer tour of South America – the Albion striker had missed a similar tour of North America organised by his club, which took in Canada, and ended with a for club tournament, won by Setubal Portugal, in Palo Alto, California.

That was not the end of Jeff's touring for the year, though, for when he reported back for training in West Bromwich in mid-July, he was immediately hauled off for a two match tour of Norway.

Albion – unusually for them, for, traditionally, they have never been a 'buying' club – had splashed out on three new players over the close season. The biggest buy was a new strike partner for Jeff, the club breaking the Albion transfer record by spending a massive £100,000 on Sunderland's bright prospect, Colin Suggett. They had strengthened the midfield by going for a proven international, Northern Ireland star Danny Hegan, who they acquired from Ipswich Town in a cash plus player deal, with Ian Collard going the other way. Then, more for the future, they had picked up Queens Park Rangers teenage midfielder Allan Glover. It was an impressive statement to the football world; Albion were not afraid to spend money to bring success to The Hawthorns, and Jeff, for one, was pleased to see some sign of ambition at the club.

Jeff got the opportunity to meet his new team mates in Norway, where all three new men got a run-out. In the first game Albion lost a tough match 3-2 against the Norwegian Under-23 side, in Bergen, on July 30, after going two goals up early on. The following day, the party moved to Oslo, where they met Norwegian champions SK Lyn Oslo, who had been drawn to meet English champions Leeds United in the first round of the European Cup. They proved little problem to Albion – or Leeds – both sides winning by the same 6-0 scoreline on Lyn's Ullevall ground. Jeff showed he had lost none of his eagerness to score goals by notching another hat-trick, in front of a sparse crowd.

Jeff played – and scored – in the only domestic warm-up game that season, a comfortable 4-0 win at Rotherham, but he knew he would be sitting out the first league game of the new campaign, because of a Football League suspension accrued from his bookings from the previous year. In his place at number nine for that opening game at the Dell was Dick Krzywicki, but filling his centre-forward role was a former lorry-driver signed from Stourbridge, Percy Freeman. The burly young-ster had a useful game – although he was no Jeff Astle, of course – and was only 'robbed' of a debut goal by the intervention of another debutant, Colin Suggett, who banged his goalbound header over the line to give Albion the lead, adding a second near the end, to give Albion a 2-0 opening day win.

On the following Tuesday, Jeff was back in the side that lost 3-1 to Coventry City at Highfield Road, but he picked up a knock that was to prove more difficult to shake off than expected, keeping him out of the next five games.

But injury was not the only problem at that time. As so often happens, Jeff's trip with the England side made him more aware of his real financial worth to the Albion. The club had a policy of paying the same basic wage to all their first team players — £60 per week. Jeff knew his Eng-land colleagues were being paid at least double that, and one day he stormed into Alan Ashman's office demanding a raise. "Some building site workers take home the same as I do. Isn't a top international footballer worth a lot more? I'm 27 and if I can't get the big money now, I never will. I'm not a money grabber but this business has been on my mind for two or three seasons. But talking to the England players on tour did accentuate the difference between me and them in terms of money. I think it's plain out of date for a club to pay everybody the same wage. If I were a medium player – and I'm not being big-headed – I'd be well satisfied, but I think I'm worth more than £60 a week."

Jeff was aware that he was challenging club policy, and never had a gripe with Ashman. "I'm not getting at the manager, because policy is policy and that's that. What I want is a change in the policy. If that doesn't happen, there's going to be a long fight, I'm afraid" – a reference to his plan to ask the club for a transfer every month until his contract ran out at the end of the season. Nor did he actually want to leave the club. "I don't want to be sold, though, even though it makes you think when you see some of the signing-on fees players who may not even succeed are getting. Good luck to them – but why should I be punished for loyalty to the club? That is what it amounts to. It's all right talking about loyalty – but you can't spend a pat on the back."

Laraine remembers discussing the issue with Jeff at the time. "Jeff never wanted to leave the Albion; it was a question of calling one's bluff. If it was a choice between Jeff asking for £100 a week, and leaving the Albion if he didn't get it, and compromising and accepting £80 a week – even though it meant that all the other top names in the First Division were getting more – then Jeff would accept the £80 a week, because he didn't want to leave the club." He always said

'I'm a Midlander through and through.' He would never have wanted to live anywhere else. Particularly London. Jeff hated big cities, and London in particular. He would have been a fish out of water anywhere else."

Eventually, a compromise was hammered out. Jeff backed down, and accepted an extra £20 a week, rather than the £40 he was demanding – but he had won the battle, for he had succeeded in changing club policy, and from then on every player coming in to the Albion negotiated his own individual salary – as at almost every big club.

Around that time Jeff and Laraine moved house, leaving the old club-house (which they had subsequently purchased) in Springfield Crescent after Laraine had passed her driving test. They moved, with the two girls, to a house in Cottesmore Close, down Pennyhill Lane, a bit off the beaten track compared to where they were before, which was within walking distance to The Hawthorns. Their new home was a self-build house, and the man who had built it had a heart attack just after finishing it. Laraine always thought that there was a bit of a jinx about the house, because of that. "All of Jeff's injuries came after we had moved into that house…"

Jeff the family man, at the new house, with Dorice, Dawn and Laraine

71

It was not until the very end of August that Jeff was ready to return to the first team. he had been much missed; the side looked rudderless in attack, as they lost to Arsenal, Coventry, Forest and Derby. In the game against Brian Clough's newly promoted side, Jeff's fans in the Birmingham Road End resorted to singing "Bring our Astle back to us," as their side missed chance after chance.

Jeff had two Reserve games, against Nottingham Forest and Wolves, and scored in both, before being catapulted back into the fray in front of 40,000 fanatical supporters at Villa Park. It was the second round of Jeff's favourite competition – the League Cup – and it provided the perfect stage for his return to the side.

Villa had got off to a bad start in the Second Division – they would end the season in the Third – but they were still drawing huge crowds. Albion took the lead early on, but after some heavy pressure, the home side scored a deserved equaliser in the 71st minute when Barry Hole stuck out a foot to deflect a Bruce Rioch free kick wide of Osborne. The Villa fans went wild at what was the first home goal scored at Villa Park that season. They were happy for just six minutes, when Fraser took a quick throw to Brown, whose shot was turned onto the bar for Astle, running in, to stoop home to head the winner. And Jeff couldn't resist running to the wall in front of the Holte End to taunt the Villa fans...

That was Jeff's first goal in what would be, after an ominous start, a tremendously rewarding season, both for him and for the Albion. But not straight away, for Jeff, who had come in for quite a hammering form Rioch in the game at Villa, was out of the next game, a 2-2 draw at struggling Sunderland. He was back for the home game with Ipswich – indeed, he would miss just one more game all season – when the club

The winning goal against Aston Villa at Villa Park...

decided to welcome him back in style, by playing the commentary from his winning goal in the 1968 FA Cup Final over the tannoy system. It was the first time that they had come up with the idea, and they would not play the clip again for another 33 years – for the first Albion FA Cup tie after Jeff's sudden death in 2002.

As usual, Jeff marked his 'home-coming' with a couple of goals, in a 2-2 draw. For the rest of the season, his form, particularly at The Hawthorns, was phenomenal; in the 22 League and Cup games that he played from then on, on home turf, he scored a staggering 23 goals. It was away from home that Jeff – and the team as a whole – struggled. Over the years, both Jimmy Hagan and Alan Ashman had, understandably, adjusted the team's tactics to accommodate their good fortune in having the best header of a ball in the country – if not the world – in the side. At The Hawthorns, that meant getting the ball forward quickly, in the air, for Jeff to head for goal, or to nod the ball down for players like Suggett or Tony Brown to pick up chances. Tactically, it worked well at The Hawthorns, where the Albion defenders and midfielders could quickly regain possession after an attack had broken down, and continue the aerial bombardment. As a result, Albion could beat the best in the First Division at The Hawthorns, as witnessed by a succession of great wins against Manchester United during Jeff's time at the club. In 1969, they beat champions Everton 2-0, whilst their nearest challengers Leeds United were fortunate to escape with a 1-1 draw.

It was never the same away from home. With home defenders constantly pushing up, it was difficult to adjust to new tactics that necessitated Jeff playing a deep-lying role. When an attack broke down, it was not so easy to regain possession, which placed considerable pressure on

...the ball's in the net, and Jeff celebrates in front of a livid Holte End

73

what was, by now, an ageing defence, and both Jeff and the team suffered. Jeff scored just seven of his thirty League and Cup goals that season away from home. In the League, the team as a whole only recorded another ten goals in the remaining sixteen games.

One of those was a classic Jeff Astle winner against Ipswich Town at Portman Road on Saturday December 13 1969. Albion won 1-0 that afternoon – but it would be another seventeen months, and 28 League games before they would win away from home again.

On November 22 1969, Jeff reached a milestone in his time with the Albion – his hundredth League goal for the club. But Jeff remembered that day for another incident, which demonstrated his relaxed relationship with manager Alan Ashman. "We all used to follow the horses at the Hawthorns — we knew all the trainers, all the jockeys. We were playing Sheffield Wednesday one day at the Hawthorns, and we had a tip on this horse, in the 2.30 race. Alan Ashman came into the dressing room to give his pre-match talk, and turned the television off, when we were watching the race. I said, 'You're not turning the television off, Alan'. 'Why's that, Jeff?' 'I've got a tip in this race and I want to see how it goes.' 'Oh, ever so sorry, Jeff'. It's true — he turned round and walked out, and we never had that pre-match talk! We beat Sheffield Wednesday 3-0 that afternoon, and I scored my hundredth League goal — but the horse came nowhere!"

Although Albion hardly set the world on fire that season in the League, they went all the way to Wembley in the League Cup – their fourth Cup Final in five years – and once again, Jeff led the charge. After scoring the winner at the Villa in the second round, he made one and scored the second in a 2-0 replay win over Ipswich Town. Although, unusually, he failed to get on the scoresheet in the 4-0 win over Bradford City in the next round, he grabbed both goals in another 2-1 replay win over Leicester City – just four days after being stretchered unconscious at Molineux, suffering from concussion.

That earned the Albion a two-legged semi-final against Alan Ashman's former club, Second Division Carlisle United, and after a 1-0 defeat at Brunton Park, Albion duly qualified for Wembley on another glorious Hawthorns winter evening, when they beat Carlisle 4-1.

The Final was not played until March, which gave Ashman a chance to address his side's poor League form. They had not managed to win a home League game until the eighth attempt, when they beat Manchester United 2-1, and with such a poor away record, home results were crucial to their survival in the top flight.

On Boxing Day, Albion entertained West Ham – the sort of game that Albion fans knew would produce a load of goals. West Ham, as usual, had their World Cup trio of Hurst, Peters and Moore in their side, but Jeff had never had problems playing against the England captain. Bobby Moore, with his boyish good looks, was the favourite of every England player's wife, and Laraine admits to a similar crush on the Golden Boy of Sixties England football. "Jeff got very friendly with Bob during his time with England, and I remember when Albion were playing West Ham in 1969, I was sitting in the old oak-paneled players' lounge at The Hawthorns and Bobby strolled in and walked straight over to me. We'd never met before, but unbeknown to me, Jeff had sent him in and told him that I liked him a lot. He came straight over to me and kissed my hand, and I was the envy of all the other players' wives. It wasn't until afterwards when Jeff told me what he'd said to Bobby that the embarrassment sank in!"

As usual, Jeff, who had long admired Moore for his ability and tough but fair play, scored one of the goals in a 3-1 win against the Hammers – but he could well have had a hat-trick, as he bemused Moore in the air throughout the game. Two weeks later, Jeff did get a hat-trick – the last of his Albion career, as it would turn out – in a thrilling 3-2 home win

100 up for Jeff, as he beats Peter Springett against Sheffield Wednesday

75

against First Division new boys Crystal Palace. Those three goals put Astle top of the First Division scoring charts, with 18 League and Cup goals, one ahead of Everton's Joe Royle, and two in front of the man regarded as Jeff's main rival for the remaining striker's role for the England World Cup squad, Peter Osgood, of Chelsea.

On January 31 Albion and Manchester City – who had beaten neighbours United in their League Cup semi-final – played a dress rehearsal for the League Cup Final at The Hawthorns, Albion winning 3-0 despite losing goalkeeper John Osborne for some of the game with a bad injury.

It would be a different story at Wembley on March 7. To start with, Albion looked very sharp against a City side playing in its first League Cup Final. They took the lead in the fifth minute when a Hope corner was headed out to Wilson. He slung the ball high to the far post where Astle outjumped the massive Corrigan in the City goal to head Albion in front. In doing so, Jeff grabbed another record that nobody will ever take away from him —

he was the first player ever to score at Wembley in both the FA Cup and the League Cup Finals.

The very early football was all Albion, but City, with Francis Lee having a magnificent game, gradually took charge. In the 20th minute Lee set up Summerbee, and Talbut had to scramble his shot off the line. Lee then had a header wide, and had another palmed over by Osborne. On the half hour Albion had their first attack for twenty minutes, when it took a brave dive by Corrigan at the feet of Astle to stop a second Albion goal.

On the strength-sapping muddy pitch, it was all

The fifth minute goal in the 1970 League Cup Final

76

And Jeff celebrates in style at Wembley

City in the second half, but Albion missed a great chance on the break to settle the tie, when Suggett streaked away only to casually stab the ball wide. The inevitable equaliser came in the 59th minute when Doyle came up on the blind side to take a Lee pass in his stride and place a firm shot just inside the post. Soon after a series of niggling fouls ended with Doyle charging Astle onto the running track, and both players were booked.

In an exciting end to the ninety minutes, Corrigan saved at the feet of Astle, Suggett hooked just over from Hope's pass, Lee shot into the side netting and Bowyer, on for the limping Summerbee, headed just over the bar. Early in the first period of extra time Krzywicki was put through by Astle, but shot wide, and that was it for Albion. In the 102nd minute of the game, Glyn Pardoe, from a Lee cross, hooked home City's winner, and Albion's dreams were dashed.

With Albion looking secure just below mid-table in the First Division, Jeff could concentrate on more personal ambitions – with England. He maintained his scoring run, with two more goals at home to Newcastle, and another in a 3-1 home win over Chelsea at Easter, when he completely upstaged Osgood, to send another message to the England manager.

On April 8 Jeff suffered the worst defeat of his professional playing career, as a very young Albion side went down 7-0 – the club's worst defeat for over sixty years – against Manchester United at a half-empty Old Trafford. Seven days later, Jeff completed his domestic season, with his thirtieth goal of the season. And what a goal it was, scored against the best goalkeeper in the world, from nearly fifty yards!

Jeff kicked off the game, against Stoke City at the Victoria Ground, and passed the ball to Asa Hartford, before moving upfield. The young Scot slipped the ball back to Jeff. "I was about 45 yards out from goal and I could hear these heavy studs pounding the turf towards me. It was Denis Smith, a real hard case, and I thought, 'Your ball Denis!'" But Jeff went for the ball, and tried an ambitious overhead kick from almost on the halfway line. The great Gordon Banks, Jeff's England colleague, was barely paying attention at such an early stage of the game – just fifteen seconds in – and was left completely stranded on the edge of his box; he could only watch, mortified, as the ball drifted over his head for a remarkable goal. It was some way to celebrate the end of the season, and a trip to Mexico, even though Stoke won the game 3-2.

That was not the end of the season for the Albion, for after a break of seventeen days, they were playing in the new Anglo-Italian competition — where, amazingly, there would be another riot, which would cause one of the games to be abandoned. This time Jeff missed it all; he was on his way to South America again, hopeful that he would make the cut for the 22-strong squad to represent England in the World Cup Finals.

A King and Three Lions

In the late 1960s, the chant "Astle for England" was heard regularly at almost every First Division game that was played at The Hawthorns. Albion's centre-forward, the undisputed King of the Brummie Road End, was banging in the goals with clockwork regularity, yet it took Jeff three full seasons before he finally achieved the call to represent his country. When it came at last, he enjoyed a brief international career which peaked in the glare of the spotlight in the World Cup in Mexico in 1970.

In retrospect, it turns out that Jeff was probably one of the unluckiest players ever to play for England. Parochially, he is the man who won the Cup for Albion; nationally, he is the man who "missed an open goal for England against Brazil in Mexico." To this day, older Baggies can still hear the mocking song, "Astle lost the World Cup" ringing in their ears, as opposing supporters took full advantage of the King's misfortune. Thus Jeff's England career is remembered for one swing of his left foot, when, in truth, there was much more to it to that... much more.

Before Astle and Brown, there was Astle and Kaye. 1965-66 was Astle's first full season at the Albion. The Baggies were a free scoring outfit who finished the season in sixth place, scoring goals all along the way. The raw-boned Astle was still learning his trade in the top flight. He had begun to get the measure of First Division defences; indeed, it was his hat-trick at Northampton – admittedly, not the acme of top flight defences – that took Albion to the top of the League on a balmy autumnal Friday in 1965.

The established star at the time, however, was centre-forward John Kaye. The Throstle's record signing from Scunthorpe was enjoying his best goalscoring season in West Bromwich. During the campaign he was twice selected for the Football League XI, scoring three times in his two outings, gradually putting himself into contention for a full England cap as the 1966 World Cup game round.

Kaye narrowly missed selection for England on two occasions; when Chelsea's Barry Bridges pipped him against Austria, in October 1965 (typical London bias), and when injury robbed him of a game against Norway in England's pre-World Cup warm-up tour of Scandinavia.

Kaye was a bustling centre-forward, a muscular front runner with good control and a powerful shot. Astle, at the time, had the edge in the air, but, in truth, few players could compete with Jeff in that particular department. Both had scored 18 goals that season, but at that time, Kaye was the better all-round player, but although Kaye made the final forty for the World Cup, he missed the cut for the final 22, and his chance was gone for ever.

In 1966-67, Kaye inexplicably lost his scoring touch, netting just five times in 40 League games, so it was just as well for Albion that Astle was ready to take up the mantle, and, with it, the coveted number nine shirt of Richardson, Walsh and Allen; a shirt that he was to make his own for the next five seasons, and forever, in the minds of thousands of Albion supporters.

There is no doubt, whatsoever, that in 1967-68, Jeff Astle was the best centre-forward in England. He was top scorer with 35 goals in League and Cup, including three hat-tricks, and in the scoring charts he was six in front of the magical George Best, and ten ahead of England's first choice Geoff Hurst. His all-round play had improved no end, so he was now almost as deadly with his right foot as he was with his famed forehead.

Yet he was not chosen for any representative game that season; not even for one of the three Football League games, when he was overlooked in favour of the likes of Frank Wignall (Forest), John Ritchie (Sheffield Wednesday) and Martin Chivers (Southampton.) Even more mystifying, after all his achievements that season, including the winner in the Cup Final, Jeff was not chosen for the England European Nations Cup squad at the season's end. Alf Ramsey was still practicing his wingless wonders formation, the nucleus of his World Cup winning squad was still intact, and he relied heavily on Hurst, and the West Ham man's almost telepathic understanding with his club colleague Martin Peters.

So, while England were battling away in the Nations Cup, Astle was with Albion in East Africa, but he felt the snub. "I was disillusioned. If I couldn't get into the England side when I was the country's top scorer, what chance would I ever have of winning a cap? In the end I reconciled myself to the fact that I would never be an England player — and banished the subject from my mind."

Jeff's position had not been totally ignored. Writing in the *Park Drive Book of Football*, Billy Wright was looking forward two years ahead to the 1970 World Cup. He selected 31 players, but only two from the Midlands. Apologising for that, he went on to say "Jeff Astle and Clive Clark have a chance to be in the Mexico party, especially if they can continue to score goals."

So, for Jeff it was business as usual at the start of the 1968-69 season. The nets bulged with goals – although not at quite the same rate as the previous season — and the local press continued to call for his selection for his country, as the "Astle for England" campaign grew and grew. Yet when the call finally arrived, nobody was more surprised that Jeff himself. He was not at all satisfied with his form at the time, because of a nagging back injury. "It was like a bolt from the blue when I turned up at Spring Road one morning and found a registered letter from the FA waiting for me. My first thought was that it was a circular or something from the disciplinary committee. The letter invited me to join England's training squad for the international against Bulgaria, at Wembley on December 11."

Jeff reported to Lancaster Gate, where he met Alf Ramsey for the first time. The call up was an exercise to get Astle involved at international level. He did not feature in the team at all. England drew 1-1, Hurst scoring the goal, but missing a boatload of chances.

But Ramsey had made a big impression on Jeff. "I had a lot of respect for Sir Alf Ramsey." At first, Jeff didn't know what to call him and after a few stutters of "Boss, gaffer, Mr Ramsey..." from Jeff, the England manager realised what the the problem was, and called Jeff to one side. "I'm Alf, Jeff – just call me Alf."

"Alf Ramsey could appear to be aloof, and distant, particularly with the press, but he was just protecting us. He was just protecting his players, and he didn't want the press sticking microphones in our faces all the time. I had a lot of time for Alf."

England's next game was against Rumania on January 15 1969, but the game clashed with Albion's vital European Cup-winners game against Dunfermline; fortunately, Ramsey appreciated the importance of the game for the Albion, and deliberately did not call on Jeff's services. Albion drew 0-0 in Scotland, England drew 1-1 at Wembley, reports saying that "England's old forward failing let them down again, and Hurst and Hunt were ineffective." It turned out to be the Liverpool star's last game for England – and the time was ripe for new blood.

The *Albion News* trumpeted developments on March 8. "Honours for Jeff Astle. He is in Sir Alf Ramsey's party for the England-France international on March 12. Well done Jeff."

Astle joined a squad of 22 for the pre-match sessions. England had scored just four goals in their last six internationals, but Astle was fit and raring to go, having missed Albion's game at Sunderland because of his call-up. There were enough hints flying around that it was to be his day – but it was not to be, as Jeff explained. "I went down with 'flu 36 hours before the game. The team was announced, and naturally I was not involved. Instead of heading for Wembley as a new international, I spent a miserable day in bed at a London hotel, cursing my bad luck."

Unfortunately for Jeff, England finally found their touch, Hurst scoring a hat-trick (including two penalties) – and Jeff may have missed out on a bean feast!

March turned out to be a dreadful month for Albion and Astle. On March 29 the Baggies missed out on Wembley when they were beaten by Leicester in the FA Cup semi-final at Hillsborough but, indirectly, the defeat gave Jeff his next call-up for "international honours" – if you could call it that.

Since 1954 the Football Association had staged a game as a curtain raiser for the FA Cup Final. On the Friday night before the big game, England took on "Young England," alternating between Stamford Bridge and Highbury. Previous fixtures had seen the likes of Don Howe, Bobby Robson and Maurice Setters participating. On April 25 1969, instead of getting ready for a second successive Cup Final, Jeff turned out for England, and his strike partner Tony Brown was a member of the Young England squad.

As the programme of the game said, "England places were up for grabs," as Astle pulled on an England shirt for the first time, albeit in a meaningless end of season shebang – and a goalless draw, on the last occasion the fixture was ever played, in front of 18,140 people at the Chelsea ground. And something good came out of it, as Jeff was selected for the end of season Home International Championship party. The real business of playing for England was just around the corner.

Traditionally, since 1872, the Home Internationals had been played through the season. In 1969, for the first time, they were all squeezed into the space of seven days, thus providing the ideal opportunity for Jeff to blend into the England scene.

Two sides of the Wales "no-goal" Jeff puts the ball into the net for England...

82

Northern Ireland were the first opposition, but Astle was a non-playing sub as England won 3-1 in Belfast, Francis Lee, Martin Peters and Geoff Hurst, from the penalty spot, scoring the goals.

On May 6 the England side were travelling by coach from the Bank of England training ground at Roehampton to the team's HQ at Hendon when Sir Alf announced the team to play Wales at Wembley the following day. Jeff was "in." There were six changes from the side that played Northern Ireland, as Jeff lined up at centre-forward alongside Francis Lee and Bobby Charlton.

The pundits harshly labelled the side as "England's second XI." That was of no consequence whatsoever to Astle, who took the field on a sunny May evening, to play in an unusually entertaining game – too often in the past this had been a very one-sided fixture. In fact, Wales took the lead through an 18th minute goal from Ron Davies, the Southampton striker who, in the League, was Jeff's only real challenger for the title of "best header of the ball in football." Minutes later, the King thought he had scored a debut goal. "The ball had swung over into the goalmouth and Rodrigues handled it. Before the referee could blow his whistle, I rammed the ball into the net." Disastrously, for Jeff, the referee disallowed the goal – and gave a penalty! With Geoff Hurst rested for the game, Francis Lee stepped up to take the spot kick, and blasted the ball against the bar.

Early in the second half, Bobby Charlton did get the ball into the Welsh net, and 18 minutes from the end Jeff was denied again. This time Alan Ball crossed from the right, Jeff met the ball powerfully with his head, only for Rodrigues (with a suspicion of handball again) and Sprake between them, to keep the ball out, right on the line. This time, though, Lee smashed the rebound home for the winning goal.

The *Football Pictorial* declared that Astle was unlucky (get away!), marking his debut thus: Marks out of ten:

...but the "goal" is disallowed — for a penalty!

6, Good tackles/interceptions: 5 Good passes: 24, Bad passes: 2, Dispossessed: 2, Goal Attempts: 5 – 1 shot disallowed, 3 headers saved, 1 header blocked on line, Chances missed: 1 shot over.

Jeff was omitted for the last game of the international series, the Blue Riband game against Scotland, when England, with a third successive win, were crowned as champions. Both Martin Peters and Geoff Hurst scored two goals in an easy 4-1 win at Wembley.

Strangely, though, Jeff returned to West Bromwich riddled with self doubt. Although he enjoyed playing for England, he confessed that he still did not feel part of the set-up, which made him feel lonely and miserable, even going so far as to confess that he would not be bothered if Ramsey left him out of future England get-togethers. Jeff felt the odd man out in the England squad. For a start, he was the only Midlander in the squad, apart from Gordon Banks, who was, of course, a long-established regular, and — literally, as a goalkeeper — probably the first name that Alf Ramsey wrote on the team sheet.

Jeff also felt left out because he was not from one of the 'glamour clubs' of Lancashire and London. Of course, Jeff knew the other members of the England squad – Osgood, the Charlton brothers, Alan Ball, and so on – but only from playing against them for Albion in the First Division, and not in any social sense.

After his first call-up with the England squad, Jeff returned home a very unhappy figure, and confided in Laraine that he would be very happy if he were never called up for the national side again.

That attitude was put to the test soon after, when it was announced that Astle had been chosen for the England party to tour South America and Mexico – vital preparation for the World Cup in South America twelve months later. Always a poor traveller, particularly as regards air travel, and reluctant to be away from home for such a long period, Jeff was close to contacting Ramsey to declare himself unavailable, and it took a great deal of persuading from Laraine to convince him that it really was in his best interests to go. "You've been the top goalscorer in the First Division for the last two years, Jeff. You might not play for Chelsea, or Manchester United, and have the press clamouring for you to go, but you've earned the right as much as anybody, and you really should go."

It was a difficult role for Laraine to play, because, more than anybody, she hated close-season tours – by Albion or England – which took Jeff away from home for weeks on end. "But I had to convince him, because I knew he would regret it in the end. You don't tell the England manager that you don't want to on tour, unless you were injured or there was a family bereavement or something. Possibly he would never play for England again, so I persuaded him to give it a try, and if it didn't get any better, then give it a miss the next time. But he enjoyed it, and he was fine going away with England after that."

Jeff was also fortunate in that his room-mate on the tour was Alan Ball. The bubbly Lancastrian was ideal company for the usually jovial Albion man , who soon settled in, and never looked back.

The tour gave Ramsey the ideal opportunity to experiment in hot humid conditions, at altitude. The opening game was a goalless draw on June 1 in Mexico City in front of 105,000 people, but Jeff was on the sidelines. Three days later Astle was selected for an England XI against a Mexican XI at Guadalajara. The match was not a full international, but it enabled Ramsey to experiment with

The Kings and the three lions — with England goalkeeper Gordon Banks

his substitutes, pushing Ball and Peters to run themselves to exhaustion to see what the heat and the altitude would do to them. They lasted into the second half, when they were replaced by Mullery and Bobby Charlton, Astle partnered Allan Clarke from the start, and both strikers scored twice in a 4-0 win.

That was Astle's only game of the tour, as England later went on to beat Uraguay 2-1 in Montevideo (Lee and Hurst) but lost to 2-1 to Brazil in Rio.

On the way home, as the team enjoyed a drink waiting for the plane, Ball and Astle treated the players to a rendition of several of the day's hits, and even Ramsey applauded the impromptu entertainment.

Jeff returned home a new man, grateful that he had heeded Larraine's advice to travel. It was up to him, now, to have a good season during 1969-70, and cement his place in the World Cup squad. Unfortunately, he got off to the worst of starts – first injuries, then a wage dispute with the Albion meant that he did not re-establish himself in the Albion side until mid-September, but after that the goals just continued to flow. England's first game of the season was against Holland on November 5 1969. Whether Jeff would have been considered or not was irrelevant, because Albion played Leicester City on that night in the League Cup, and Jeff scored the two goals that helped Albion nearer to Wembley again. A month later Ramsey announced the squad for the game against Portugal at Wembley on December 10; Jeff was in the squad, and made the starting line-up for his second cap. The match programme recorded that "Astle had been capped against Wales earlier in the year,

More bad luck with England — brought down by the Portuguese keeper

86

and was particularly dangerous in the air." It was the shortest of all the pen-pictures.

The only goal of the game came from Jack Charlton, heading home a corner taken by his brother. Jeff had a quiet game – but was involved in the most controversial incident of the game. Early in the second half he had a shot blocked on the line by Cardoso. With twenty minutes to go Peters sent Astle clear on goal; he rounded the keeper and looked set to score his first full international goal, until the keeper pulled him down in the box – penalty! Francis Lee, despite his miss from the spot in Astle's first game, was entrusted with the kick. And yes, he missed again!

Jeff was called up again for the return game against Holland At Wembley, but had to pull out through injury. That let in another one of Jeff's First Division rivals, Leeds striker Mick Jones, but although he played well, a goalless draw did no harm to Jeff's overall chances.

In February, it was Belgium away. Astle travelled, but played no part in the game; his closest rival in the scoring charts that season, Peter Osgood, of Chelsea, made his debut, and starred in a 3-1 win, although it was Alan Ball and Geoff Hurst who got on the scoresheet. It soon became obvious that Jeff's main rival for the

Even with England, it's Jeff who leads the card school on tour

centre-forward spot was the Kings Road boy, the darling of the London press, and their choice for Mexico.

For Jeff, there was one more chance to shine before the Home Internationals at the end of the season, when, as the First Division's top scorer, Jeff lined up for the Football League against the Scottish League at Highfield Road on March 18 1970. Osgood was left out this time, as Jeff partnered Brian Kidd, and took his chance well, scoring two goals in a 3-2 win, with a certain Willie Johnston, of Rangers, scoring for the Scots.

Astle had done enough, and his name was there when the initial 28 for Mexico was announced; he would definitely be travelling,

Jeff in the thick of it against Scotland at Hampden Park

but there was still a further excision to be made, to reduce the squad for 22 for the final matches themselves.

As Jeff reflected later, "Outside the Midlands few professional observers had rooted for my selection, and the reaction in most national newspapers when it was announced was cool. It was clear that most of them assumed that I would be one of the six to be axed."

At the season's end Astle was nce again the top scorer in Division One, and had 25 League goals to his credit. His nearest rival was Peter Osgood, with 23, with Allan Clarke on 17, Geoff Hurst 16 and Brian Kidd 11. The King had done as much as he could to secure his place in Mexico – now it was down to Ramsey.

The England squad took part in the Home Internationals. They drew 1-1 with Wales in Cardiff, with Jeff's former Albion colleague Dick Krzywicki scoring the opening goal for the Welshmen and beat Northern Ireland 3-1 at Wembley, a game which saw Brian Kidd's debut, as well as being Bobby Charlton's 100th cap. That left just one more game before Mexico, against Scotland – and Jeff was chosen for England's showpiece international of the season, at Hampden Park on April 25 1970.

Unfortunately, by his own admission, he had a poor game, hardly touching the ball in the ninety minutes, but he was not on his own, as the Scots dominated a encounter which ended as the first goalless draw between the two countries since they played the

The benefits of being a World Cup star — Jeff picks up his car from Ford

first-ever soccer international 98 years before.

As Albion played in the first Anglo-Italian tournament, Jeff flew out to Mexico with high expectations, and World Cup fever hit the UK in a big way. The squad all received cars – although only on a year's loan — from the Ford Motor Company. When Jeff jumped at the chance to buy the car, at a discount, a year later, Ford wrote back, confiding that they had had an enormous amount of trouble getting the cash – or the cars back – from the rest of the squad, all of whom were earning significantly more than Jeff!

They made a hit single and LP, with Back Home, Findus used them to advertise fish fingers and Esso issued a series of collectable World Cup coins, each with a different player. Astle was included, thus becoming the first (and only) Albion player to feature on a coin. Where better to put the head of a king? Jeff was less than impressed with his likeness – "It was nothing like me!" Every player featured on the coins – and they were issued before the final cull, so there were more than the bare 22 – received a beautiful sterling silver presentation version of the full set.

And Jeff wasn't just featured at petrol stations. Robertson issued a series of jams with the England World Cup players' faces on the lids, and Laraine can remember foraging through the jam section at Tescos in West Bromwich looking for a Robertson's lid with Jeff's face beaming from it. She was unsuccessful, because what football fan in West Bromwich had not also gone through the same procedure to make sure they got a picture of their Albion footballing hero?

The players met at Heathrow Airport on May 4 for the fourteen hour flight to the soccer adventure of a lifetime. The first fortnight involved fitness training and some relaxation, after which Ramsey arranged a two week tour in Columbia and Ecuador. On May 18 the England squad visited Bogota, where the much documented Bobby Moore bracelet saga took place. Jeff was more concerned about making that last 22. The deadline for that decision was May 23, but before that, on the 20th, England had two games. England 'B' would meet Columbia 'B' to be followed by a meeting between the full sides later in the day.

To his dismay, Astle was named only as one of the two subs for the 'B' team. As he kicked his heels on the bench, the England "Stiffs" stuttered, but with twenty minutes to go, he came on for Brian Kidd and five minutes later a cross came over, Colin Bell helped it on, and Jeff prodded home the winner. A classic case of being in the right place at the right time.

Three days later came the news that Jeff was desperate to hear, as Sir Alf announced the unfortunate six to go home – and Jeff was not one of them! Jeff had thought that, in particular, Peter Osgood, being from a more fashionable club, would get to Mexico ahead of him – but Alf picked both of them, as the First Division top scorers that season, whilst their fellow striker, Manchester United's Brian Kidd, ended up on the plane back home.

On May 24, the England 'B' side played again – with a 9.30 am kick-off – against an Ecuador University side. Astle played the full game, and with a weight lifted off his shoulders, had a blinder, as England won 4-1. He scored all four goals – one deflected into the net off Emlyn Hughes, but Sir Alf insisted that Jeff claim it.. The full England team then beat Ecuador 2-0 with Brian Kidd – ironically one of the six going home – scoring one of the goals.

If Bobby had been having problems because of the Bogota incident, then Jeff's return flight to Mexico City was another nightmare. All of the players were given sleeping tablets to help them cope with the awkward overnight flight. Astle delayed taking his, with disastrous results; he hated flying anyway, so what happened on that trip must have been truly terrifying.

Somewhere between Panama and Mexico City, there was a violent electrical storm. The plane was tossed around in the air and

The official send off for Mexico — Jeff waves with Banks, Newton and Ball

lightning flashed all around. Jeff was still wide awake, as clouds of what appeared to be smoke started to seep from the cabin (it turned out to be a new anti-condensation device) and everyone thought the plane was on fire.

As the situation gradually abated, and the weather improved, one of the stewardesses gave Jeff a drink – he thought whisky or brandy – and he gulped it down, on top of the sleeping pills, which were now just starting to do their job!

When the plane landed in Mexico City, as the tablets kicked in, Jeff got to the waiting lounge – and collapsed! The Mexican press, who had been looking for any excuse to vilify the England party after the Bogota affair, seized the opportunity to get photographs of the dishevelled Astle, sprawled across the luggage, which were transmitted around the world, with the captions telling their own, inaccurate story, "England arrive drunk and incomplete."

As for Jeff – he remembered nothing of the incident, and woke the next day to read the headlines, and be staggered by the publicity his fear of flying had generated.

Back in England, Laraine Astle was furious when she saw the headlines. She explained to the *Birmingham Evening Mail*, who arranged for her to telephone her husband in Mexico. "Jeff really dislikes flying, and was usually green when he got off a plane. And he wasn't drunk. He might have the odd pint, but he has always hated the taste of spirits. It's a good job I wasn't there; I'd give them something to think about!" Astle himself dismissed the allegations as "scandalous", after the England team doctor diagnosed "acute air sickness."

For Ramsey, enough was enough; there was even unprecedented talk of the holders withdrawing from

Jeff is checked over by a worried England physio, Les Cocker, at Mexico City airport

92

the World Cup and, in the words of Alan Hubbard in the *Daily Sketch*, "leaving the Mexicans to stew in their own bean soup."

Fortunately, things cooled down and England remained to defend their trophy. Astle recovered from his air sickness to become the life and soul of the party. Peter Osgood recalled that "Jeff was a very funny man, who helped keep the players' spirits high." It is now a well-known tale that Jeff took a portable record player with him, and drove everybody daft by playing Norman Greenbaum's *Spirit in the Sky* over and over again. Eventually, Osgood and Hurst, between them, smashed the disc out of desperation.

"Back Home," the Astles admire Jeff's cap against Czechoslovakia

England's World Cup campaign kicked off on June 2, against Rumania. Jeff played no part in the game, and Geoff Hurst scored the only goal of the game in the 65th minute.

The next game was the one the whole world had been waiting for since the groups were first drawn, as the holders faced the favourites – Brazil – at the Jalisco Stadium in Guadalajara, on Sunday June 7. Expectations were high for a match that many would have wanted as the Final, and the pundits were not disappointed.

The great Brazilian side had a wealth of talent, with skill, flair, pace, ball control and, of course, Pele. If ever there was a classic contest between the traditional English game and the artistry of South America, this was it. The game had everything. Moore versus Pele, the greatest save that the best goalkeeper in the world, Gordon Banks, would ever make, 65,000 fervent fans and, last but not least, an appearance by the Black Country's finest, Jeff Astle, whose lot it was to make a lasting impression in arguably one of the most fascinating World Cup Final games ever played.

Jeff started the game on the bench. At half time there was no score, but England had more than held their own in the torrid conditions. When the second half began, Brazil started to turn the screw, but the England defence held firm until the 60th minute when Pele set up Jairzinho to hammer the ball past Banks. Ramsey decided to change his tactics, bringing on Astle and Bell for Lee and Charlton, to attack the suspect Brazilian defence in the air.

No sooner had Jeff stepped on the pitch – all hot and bothered off the bench – that a chance came his way. His first touch, though, was to head down a cross for Alan Ball to miss his kick ten yards out. Them crucially, a defensive mix-up left him clear, twelve yards out, with just Felix to beat.

Before Jeff was called upon, he was actually close to nodding off in the tremendous heat that the substitutes were suffering in on the bench — Emlyn Hughes had to rouse him from near slumber before he entered the field of play. Whether he was wide awake or not, the chance which fell to him was one which he would have scored nine times out of ten, and Jeff knew it. "I had all the time in the world. I could have brought the ball up to the goalkeeper and just slipped it past him. Instead, I blasted at the ball straight away, and hit it past the far post."

Millions were watching the game around the world – and Albion fans around the Black Country, watching the game on their television screens, groaned with disappointment. Late on Astle set up Ball again, who hit the bar – a chance every bit as bad as Jeff's. in retrospect — as England eventually lost 1-0. The inquest went on long through the night. Poor Jeff. "I could have cried when I saw the ball go past the post," he said later; the irony was, the 27 minutes he played in the Mexican heat were the best he played in an England shirt, for the Brazilian defence, not sturdy in the air at the best of times, quaked with fear every time a cross was launched towards Astle.

Jeff started the next game against Czechoslovakia when Hurst was rested and Allan Clarke made his debut alongside him. In the 49th minute England were awarded a penalty and with Lee and Hurst out of the side, Clarke kept his cool to mark his debut with a goal.

Jeff didn't complete the game, being withdrawn in favour of Osgood, as England won 1-0 to qualify for the quarter finals. Jeff later wrote about his final England game. "The least said about my performance the better. It was easily my worst in representative football. I kept jumping under the ball; no doubt the thin air had something to do with it. But, in all honesty, it was a case of being very off form." Jeff had noticed that the thin air in Mexico City – at an altitude of well over a mile – was seriously affecting his ability to time his jump for the ball. "I would jump for where I would expect the ball to be in England, and when I got up to meet it, it would have gone, moving through the air faster than I was used to."

In the quarter-final, against West Germany in Leon, England – with Jeff not playing – notoriously blew a 2-0 lead as Bonetti let in three and the holders crashed out. In the end, though, Jeff had the consolation – such as it was — that his miss against Brazil had just cost England the draw, not the World Cup, for even with the extra point England would STILL have finished second in their group, and would STILL have met the Germans. Of course, had that shot gone in against the Brazilians, Jeff might well have started against West Germany, and who knows what might have happened then...

On June 16 the England party flew home, and Jeff ruminated on the experience, and the fact that he had played in one of the "great" World Cups, against one of the best teams of all time, the ultimate champions in 1970, Brazil.

He made his final representative appearance in September 1970, when the Football League played the Irish League at Carrow Road, Norwich, and he joined his pal and Albion clubmate Tony Brown in the side. In the match programme on the night it said, "Jeff has become one of the deadliest finishers in the game, and his value in the transfer market must be near-astronomical." He lived up fully to the billing, scoring twice, and setting up another for Bomber Brown as well. Reports said that the Astle-Brown combination tore the Irish apart.

For the rest of the season in the First Division, Jeff turned very much from goal scorer, to goal provider, as Tony Brown swept to the top of the scoring charts just as Astle had done the year before. At least Jeff left the representative stage on a goalscoring note.

Whether Jeff really did suffer because of the World Cup is questionable. He was never allowed to forget THAT miss, even though it did not really matter in the end. In a perfect world, Jeff Astle should have played for England at the end of the 1967-68 season, when he was the best player in his position in the country. Had that happened, by the time Mexico came round, he would have been well established in the side, and as for that miss against Brazil – well, who knows...

That is all romantic speculation. The harsh reality is that the miss against Brazil did blight Astle's career. A close look at his representative games makes interesting reading. In his six minor matches, he scored eleven goals (if you give him all four against the Liga University side in Ecuador). In his five full England games he had a goal disallowed, had three efforts cleared off the line, and was denied a certain goal by that foul by Henrique, the Portuguese goalkeeper. In his twelve appearances in an England shirt, he was only on the losing side once – against three times World Champions Brazil. That is not a bad record in anybody's books, and the facts prove pretty conclusively that Jeff had nothing to be ashamed of in his England career.

In these days of marketing and ultra-commercialisation, players who miss vital World Cup deciding penalties actually make money out of it. Gareth Southgate, Stuart Pearce, David Batty and Chris Waddle are lucky. Their misses actually cost England dear, but they made light of it by selling pizzas, and won the public sympathy. In 1970, things were very different – but now the great man is gone, it is time to forget the Brazil miss and simply reflect on how good a player Jeff Astle was, for both club and country. Truly a King amongst the Three Lions.

Picking up the pieces, 1970-71

Jeff reported back to The Hawthorns after the excitement – and the disappointment – of Mexico, in July 1970. He was fit – but had he been affected by the miss against Brazil, and would be bothered by the inevitable barracking that he would receive from non-Albion fans in the First Division? At first, it appeared not, and he was able to brush off the incident with the usual Astle jokey aside. "Afterwards I found that I had my laces tied together when I missed that one," or, "I didn't miss the one at Wembley, did I?" — which was Jeff's way of defusing it. He never appeared bothered about it when people brought it up. But there was little doubt that his play suffered, as he admitted to his wife. "You would have to be devoid of all feelings for it not to affect you. Jeff would come home after a game and say to me that it had some effect. But he hid it very well, and it pleased him to respond to the barracking by scoring a goal."

His first games for Albion after Mexico were in two pre-season friendlies, at home to Scottish side Hearts, and away to Third Division Aston Villa, and in neither game did Jeff display the form that he had shown at the end of the previous season. He seemed slow, lacking in confidence, and less effective than usual in the air.

The new League season was due to kick off with a home game against Crystal Palace, but Alan Ashman was so concerned about Jeff's form that he played Jeff in a Reserve team friendly against Southern League side Worcester City. "With five days to go to the new season, I am not satisfied with Jeff's form; and neither is he," said Ashman. "In two pre-season matches, hesitation and

Back on the scoring trail at Bloomfield Road

lack of confidence have cost him three goals that he would normally score with his eyes shut. He has been crucified for missing that easy chance in the World Cup. Ever since he came home he has carried that moment around with him like a lead weight and people point him out as 'the man who missed the sitter.' It's obviously praying on his mind, and from my point of view, it would have been better if he'd never gone to Mexico."

Ashman had travelled to the World Cup Finals, and seen all of England's games, and more. "I've told Jeff that I saw world-class players, including Pele, miss easier chances in Mexico, but it's proving a difficult job to remove the unmerciful hammering he has taken." The Reserves won 3-0 at Worcester's St George's Road ground, and Jeff was on target at last, with one of the goals, but once again he gave another unconvincing display, with only two shots and one header at goal all game.

And things were little better against Palace. Ashman kept faith with his star striker, but the result was a disappointing goalless draw, and again, Jeff was a shadow of his former self. Four days later, at the City Ground, Nottingham, the situation looked equally grim, for Albion were 3-1 down to Forest with five minutes to go, after another poor performance. A few minutes before, referee John Gow had overruled the linesman's flag to award Forest a goal that was clearly offside. Stung by such a poor decision, Albion fought back. In the 85th minute Jeff wandered out to the right wing before lashing over a cross for Tony Brown to score, and three minutes later, Jeff stole up on the blind side to bundle home Tony's left wing corner to score his first goal of the season, and grab an unexpected point.

Once the floodgates had opened, it may have seemed to the external observer as if Jeff was back on form. He certainly was back on the goal standard. In the next game, against newly promoted Blackpool at Bloomfield Road, Jeff opened the scoring in the second minute, when he put home a cross from Len Cantello, but the Seasiders, inspired by a marvellous performance from Fred Pickering, won the game 3-1.

Jeff scored another second minute goal four days later, in the home game against Stoke City. Once again, as with his last goal against Gordon Banks, it was something special – but in a very different way – as he got his backside in the way of Banks' drop-kick. As the ball ran loose, Jeff got to it first, rounded the England keeper, and rolled the ball into the net, and despite all the protests of the City defenders, claiming 'foot up' on the keeper, the referee gave the goal. Albion went on to win an entertaining game 5-2, with Jeff concluding the scoring when he put away a Suggett pass a minute from the end.

Still the scoring continued. The Stoke match was the start of a run of three consecutive home games – and Jeff scored in all three. On the Saturday Liverpool came to town, and looked to be going away with both points – until Jeff popped up to capitalise on a Tommy Smith error, firing home an unstoppable shot from the edge of the area to earn a 1-1 draw. It was Jeff's best performance of the season, and but for the performance of young keeper Ray Clemence, he would have had a hat-trick.

Alan Ashman's analysis of Albion's so far stuttering start to the season was that Jeff was lacking sufficient service from the wings – something which had been a problem ever since Clive Clark had left the club the year before. The manager looked to his former side, Carlisle United, and bought winger George McVitie for £30,000, and gave him his debut in the next game, at home to Newcastle United. It was also a special day for Jeff, who was made team captain by Ashman. "Astle has been third choice skipper because Doug Fraser and John Kaye were both injured. I've been impressed with the way Jeff has led the team in the last three games, scoring four goals and thriving on the extra responsibility. Now I've made him captain because when Kaye and Fraser return to the side I don't want them to have that extra burden. I think it will make Jeff an even better centre-forward."

And the new partnership got off to a great start when, in the 14th minute McVitie beat two players in a mazy run down the

Jeff heads home new winger McVitie's cross against Newcastle in 1970

left wing before crossing superbly for Astle to head a classic goal past McFaul, at the near post. It was Astle's sixth goal of the season, but, significantly, the first with his head. Unfortunately, a game which had started so well, ended so badly.

Keith Dyson equalised for United, and three minutes from time, Albion lost a game that they dominated, when full-back Ray Wilson scored a disastrous and comical own goal past Jim Cumbes. McVitie was disappointed with the result, but was looked forward to setting up many more Astle goals. "It is wonderful to know that there is someone in the middle with the ability of Jeff Astle who can turn a bad centre into a good one."

The defeat against Newcastle was the Albion's first at home in almost a year. Away from home it was a different story, as the side came in for some real hammerings; 4-1 at Maine Road, 3-0 at Selhurst Park and, worst of all, 6-2 at Highbury. Jeff was still scoring goals, with one in a 2-2 draw at Ipswich, as, for the second time that season he inspired his side to come back from a two goal deficit, and another, the opening goal, in a 3-0 demolition of champions Everton.

He also scored another in a 3-1 League Cup win over Second Division Charlton, as Albion maintained their astonishing one hundred percent home record in that competition. That was Jeff's 19th goal in the League Cup, a cumulative record which still stands at the Albion – and with the reduced number of games played in the competition, it is a record that is likely to stand for all time. There would be no repeat of the previous year's Wembley appearance though, as Albion went out 5-0 in a wretched display at eventual winners Tottenham, in the fourth round.

In the first half of the season, Jeff managed to score nine goals in the League; a desperately poor return by his standards, although his scoring run earned him a call-up by Sir Alf Ramsey for the Football League side against the Irish League at Carrow Road. In that game, his last representative game for his country, Jeff came up with the goods again, scoring two goals in a 5-0 win.

In the second half of the season, though, it would be even worse for Jeff, with just four more goals in the League and one in the FA Cup, and the total of fifteen goals was by far the worst return of his Albion career to date, especially considering that he only missed one first team game – at home to Manchester City – all season.

Fortunately for the Albion, another goalscorer was coming through to take his place – in as much as anybody could take the place of Jeff Astle. Tony Brown took over Jeff's mantle as the First Division's top scorer with 28 League goals (plus two in the FA Cup) and, as Jeff's career at the Albion began a nose-dive, it was his close friend – Jeff had been his best man at Tony's wedding – who would become Albion's one-man goal production line for the next eight years. Not without a certain amount of help from Jeff – his headed flicks and lay-offs would be responsible for setting up a fair few of the 'Bomber's' goals that season.

Off the pitch, Jeff had joined the increasing numbers of top footballers to tell their story – although he was only the second Albion star, after Ronnie Allen, to write a book — with the publication of *Striker!*, ghost-written by journalist Philip Osborn, and published by Pelham Books, at thirty shillings. Far superior to similar publications of the time, it covered Jeff's career to date, including a chapter on Mexico, and sold very well amongst his many fans. At the same time, on the commercial side, Jeff also had his own 'Jeff Astle boots' on sale in the shops, at 69/6d, as befitted a player as much in the limelight as Jeff.

In January 1971, Jeff scored what would prove to be his last goal for Albion in a competition which had done much to make

Jeff in print — he and Laraine peruse his autobiography, Striker!

his name – the FA Cup. Albion had been drawn at home to Fourth Division Scunthorpe United in the third round, but they had struggled badly against a side that featured the young Kevin Keegan, and were fortunate to come away with a goalless draw.

In the replay on January 11, at the Old Show Ground, Scunthorpe gave another great display and took an early lead, only for Albion to fight back and win 3-1. Tony Brown scored the first two goals and Jeff took scoring leave of a competition that he had graced with a goal in the 64th minute when he headed a Lovett cross on to Brown, who controlled the ball before slipping it back to his captain, Astle shooting low into the net. As in the League Cup and the Texaco Cup (Albion went out in the first round to Scottish side Greenock Morton) there was to be no cup run; Albion went out 3-0 to Ipswich Town in a fourth round replay at Portman Road.

That replay saw the last Albion outing for one of Jeff's Cup-winning colleagues from 1968, John Talbut, who would take up a player-manager position with Belgian side FC Mechelen, at the end of the season. Realising that he was in charge of an ageing side, Ashman was gradually trying to replace the old guard, and bring in new blood. He had already sold another Cup winner, Doug Fraser, to Nottingham Forest, whilst his captain Graham Williams had finished his playing career, and had taken up a position as assistant manager.

A classic Astle header puts Albion ahead at Goodison Park

A 4-1 thrashing at Stamford Bridge followed on hard after the cup defeat, and Ashman called his players together for crisis talks before the home game against relegation-threatened Burnley at The Hawthorns. And some honest talking seemed to work wonders. Albion beat Burnley, to ease any relegation worries that they had themselves, and their away form began to improve as well. In their next away game after that players' meeting, Albion led 2-1 until the last minute at White Hart Lane, only to concede two penalties (on of which was missed by Alan Mullery) and draw 2-2. Then, two weeks later, at Goodison Park, Albion raced into a two goal lead in the first eight minutes, with Jeff opening the scoring with a classic header, only to see themselves losing 3-2, and it took a late goal from Talbut's replacement, John Wile, to earn another away point.

They even managed a superb 1-1 draw at Anfield, in a game brought forward 24 hours to avoid clashing with the Grand National, but that away win was proving very elusive. On Good Friday morning, at Upton Park, they led for much of the game thanks to another Astle goal, only to concede an equaliser to 'Pop' Robson, and an 86th winner to Jimmy Greaves – the final and 357th League goal of his glittering career.

Only once in their history – in 1891-2, when they lost ten and drew three of their thirteen games – had Albion played an entire season without winning away from home in the League, but with three tough away trips remaining, at Leeds, Newcastle and Derby, it looked as if history would be repeated.

When the team travelled to Leeds on April 17 1971, few people would have bet on them to break their duck at Elland Road. Leeds were a marvellous team at that time. League champions – and League Cup winners — in 1969, and runners-up in both League and FA Cup in 1970, they were pressing hard for honours again in the Fairs Cup and the League in 1971. Their side was full of flair players – Allan Clarke, Eddie Gray, Peter Lorimer and Johnny Giles – but also had more of its share of hard men, like Norman Hunter and Jack Charlton. They were a formidable side that rarely lost in front of their fanatical home crowd, although they had shown signs of weakness a few months before by sensationally losing an FA Cup tie at Fourth Division Colchester. However, when Albion arrived in Leeds they were top of the First Division, where they had been for almost all of the season, a couple of points ahead of rivals Arsenal, and they had only lost four games all season.

They were featured that morning on the *BBC's Football Focus* programme, when Johnny Giles foolishly declared that the game "was a good opportunity to boost Leeds' goal difference, which could prove important in the title race with Arsenal." That was a mistake, for the Albion players were watching the programme in their hotel before they left for the ground. The programme did what Alan Ashman was becoming increasingly incapable of doing – it wound the players up.

In an extraordinary game, Albion got off to a sizzling start. Hartford shot just wide of the far post, then it took a great tackle from Hunter to stop Astle running clear. In the 18th minute Albion, playing their best football of the season, went ahead when Charlton presented the ball straight to Astle and he sent Suggett away on the right. Tony Brown, named the same day as *Midlands Player of the Year*, ran into the open space to collect the ball on the right of the area, then beat Sprake with a low shot on the near post.

It should have been two after 31 minutes, when a long ball from Hope sent Suggett clear; after beating Hunter he shot against Sprake who had dashed a long way out of goal to clear.

Twice in the first five minutes of the second half Albion could have added to their score. In the 48th minute John Wile grazed the crossbar with a fine header; two minutes later a brilliant break and pass inside from Suggett let in Brown. Sprake stopped the first shot with his foot, and when the ball came back to

Referee Ray Tinkler is ushered away by the players as the Leeds fans riot in 1971

104

Brown, he hit a tame shot straight at the Welsh keeper.

In the 53rd minute Jones got the ball into the Albion net, but it was disallowed for pushing, then, as Leeds started to get into their stride at last, Cumbes saved a Clarke back-header and a Giles shot.

In the 69th minute, Albion, incredibly, scored again. Tony Brown intercepted a poor Hunter pass, to race clear of a Leeds defence that was completely stretched. The home defenders all stopped, desperately appealing for offside because Colin Suggett was still ambling back from a previous attack. However, although the linesman flagged, referee Ray Tinkler decided that as Brown had not actually made a pass forward – the ball had just bounced off him as he made the interception – then Suggett's position was irrelevant, and play was waved on. An incredulous Brown raced on fifty yards before slipping the ball forward to Astle – who could well have been offside – who rolled the ball joyously into the net.

As the Leeds players – and manager Revie, who walked onto the pitch to join in – complained, spectators ran onto the pitch to try to attack the referee, and one of the linesmen was hit by a missile and had to receive treatment.. Fighting broke out in the home end and many arrests were made and it was several minutes before the game could be restarted, after the police had lined up in a line along the Leeds end to prevent any further pitch invasions. The scenes were unlike any ever witnessed at a British football ground.

The rest of the game consisted of constant Leeds attacks against a resolute Albion defence, but it was not until the 88th minute that Allan Clarke pulled a goal back for the home side. Even worse for Leeds was the fact that Arsenal had won 1-0 against Newcastle at Highbury, putting them top of the First Division on goal difference, with two games in hand.

When time had been allowed for the angry crowd to disperse. the Albion players got back on the team coach, cock-a-hoop with the win, but all they got from chairman Jim Gaunt was a gruff "It was a pity you couldn't have done it 17 months ago."

After the event, both Revie and his players – and Johnny Giles in particular – blamed Albion for "wasting nine months of hard work," as Arsenal crept back to the top of the table in the last match of the season to win the League by a single point. In fact, they cost Leeds considerably more. As a result of the near riot, the Football Association closed down Elland Road for the first four games of the following season. Leeds Although Leeds beat Newcastle 5-1 at Hillsborough, and Crystal Palace 2-0 at Huddersfield, they dropped two points in games that they would have been expected to win at Elland Road, drawing 1-1 with Tottenham at Hull, and 0-0 with Wolves at Leeds Road. At the end of the 1971-72 season, they missed out on the championship once again, by a solitary point to Derby County...

Jack Charlton always remembered the goal that effectively cost Leeds United two championships. Years later, when he was doing the after dinner circuit at the Belfry in Birmingham, he caught sight of Jeff in the audience, and broke off his talk, to point and joke – "That bastard cost us the championship — twice!" Jeff was not so non-plussed as to call out, "You have to play to the whistle Jack – so it wasn't offside."

If was a significant goal for Jeff as well – it was not only his final goal of the season; it was the last he would score for the Albion for seven months, the most barren spell of his career so far.

The season ended in more controversy for Jeff, when he was relieved of the club captaincy, in favour of John Kaye, for "giving unauthorised interviews to the press," in which he had rashly claimed that he had made over £200 from selling FA Cup Final tickets three years before. The huge publicity which the interview received started an Football Association investigation which ended with Jeff being fined £100, and banned from receiving Cup Final tickets.

Laraine thought the affair was blown up out of all proportion. "It was taken out of context. Jeff had his brothers and sisters – and their partners and his Mom and Dad, so he never had any spare tickets to sell. That incident taught Jeff to realise who his friends in the press really were. All Jeff said was that if he had bought Cup Final tickets for a fiver, and someone came along and offered him a tenner, then he would sell them. Well, who wouldn't do that? But he wasn't actually selling tickets at all. It was ridiculous."

Alan Ashman was disappointed with the way things had turned out. "This has been a very difficult few days for us all. It is not easy taking the captaincy from one player and handing it to another. Astle appreciates and accepts the situation that has arisen and has reacted very well to it. It has been a particularly difficult time for him." There were more difficult times ahead for both Astle and Ashman.

Last years in West Bromwich

In the summer of 1971, rumours were rife that Brian Clough, then still manager of Derby County, and a long time admirer, was interested in taking Jeff to the Baseball Ground, and Clough and Taylor were seen at Spring Road. However, although Ashman discussed the approach with his directors, the Albion boss was reluctant to part with his star, at least until he had a replacement. At one point, Jeff told his brother Ken that he would be a Derby player "within two days," but nothing happened, and Jeff and his family (along with Tony and Irene Brown) and Alan Ashman went their separate ways on holiday.

On June 20 1971, the press got hold of the story that Ashman was about to be replaced as manager by ex-Albion star Don Howe. Disgracefully, Ashman learned of his sacking from a Greek waiter whilst on holiday in Rhodes. Meanwhile, Don Howe was enjoying his break in Santa Posa, whilst chairman Jim Gaunt was in Borth, north Wales. Derby took advantage of the situation to table a bid of £100,000 for Jeff, and were promised that Gaunt would finalise the deal when he returned from holiday. The rest of the board had already taken the decision to sell, and were waiting to ratify the decision with Gaunt and the incoming Don Howe. Ashman had still had no official contact from the club, and spoke to the local press from Rhodes, "I'm not surprised that there has been a bid for Astle. What bothers me is that I still have no idea what is going on."

Jeff was on holiday in Spain, watching the series of events unfold in the press. When he learned that Howe was taking over, he was fatalistic. "I thought back to a game against Arsenal at The Hawthorns not long after I joined the Albion. Don Howe was playing full-back and I clattered him into the tunnel in the old Halfords Lane Stand, and I could still remember the look he gave me..." Jeff turned to Laraine and said, "That's me finished at the Albion!"

Howe took over at The Hawthorns on July 9 1971, and he immediately issued a statement to the press regarding Jeff's future at the club, which brought to an end any chance that Jeff might have had to join Derby – who would win the First Division Championship the following year. "The immediate future of World Cup striker Jeff Astle is at The Hawthorns. There have been reports that Astle was leaving but my attitude is that he is a fine player who can still do a good job for Albion – and, indeed, England. I shall chat with him when the players report back and I hope to see him settle down and do well here." Don Howe had been a popular player at The Hawthorns, a classy full-back who had won 23 consecutive caps for England, but moved to Arsenal for a club record fee of £45,000 in 1964, after clashing with Jimmy Hagan. He had joined the Highbury coaching staff after a broken leg had prematurely ended his playing career, and had made his name there as coach under Bertie Mee, as the Gunners won the League and Cup Double in 1971.

His return as manager was, initially, a very popular move; but not everyone was happy. Jeff was not impressed with his style, or his tactical plans. "Howe told me that I was burning poor Tony Brown out. He's told me to stop heading the ball, and to shield it and bring others into the play, like Geoff Hurst does. I told him that if he wanted me to stop heading the ball, he would be best getting rid of me!"

Howe tried to turn Albion into a second Arsenal, adopting a more methodical approach to the game, with discipline and organisation the keywords. It was a far cry from Albion's traditional attacking flair, and it would see the number of goals drop dramatically – and the number of fouls and bookings rise substantially.

Ironically, Howe's first games in charge were in the Watney Cup, a pre-season competition that Albion had qualified for because of their goal scoring the previous season under Ashman. They kicked their way to the Final with wins at Wrexham and Halifax (where the local newspaper pointed out a foul ratio of 31-10 against the Albion, plus four bookings) to earn a home Final against a Colchester side captained by one of Jeff's former team mates, Bobby Cram.

The match, unlike so many that awful, awful season, was a real thriller, and at the end of normal time the game was set at 4-4, Jeff scoring twice, including a last gasp equaliser at the Birmingham Road End. The trophy was decided on penalties, and Albion lost 4-3 (Hope, Brown and Astle

Jeff in an unusual stance, smashing a penalty past Colchester's Graham Smith

scoring from the spot) with Cantello and Ray Wilson the villains of the piece, blazing their efforts over the bar.

When the season started in earnest, Albion got off to a good start, with opening wins over West Ham and Everton – but there was a complete change of style, with the opening attacking play that the club had been renowned for being replaced by a tough, aggressive style of play. Jeff played in the first four games, then missed two matches with stomach pains, before returning for the home game with Arsenal – which saw the 'Imitation Gunners' beaten 1-0 at home. Jeff's form had not been good – but he had an excuse, for a week later, he was rushed into hospital for an operation to remove an appendix that had been troubling him, misdiagnosed, for some time. While he was recuperating, Howe signed a former Arsenal colleague, Bobby Gould, supposedly to team up with Jeff as a striking pair.

With Albion performing dismally, Jeff was rushed back too early, for the game on October 9 at Crystal Palace. He was glad to be back, though. "I would like to thank the hundreds of people who sent me get-well messages. I feel fine now, and I am surprised to be back in action so soon. I am grateful to our club surgeon, and the hospital, nurses and club staff who have made it possible."

And the Albion were pleased to have him back; the 2-0 win at Selhurst Park was their first in ten games. However, by the end of the month Jeff was dropped, and on October 30 played in the Reserves alongside Jim Cumbes, Lyndon Hughes, Bobby Hope, John Kaye and Colin Suggett, all of whom had started the season in the first team.

With so much talent in the side, the Central League game against Preston drew over 3,000 to The Hawthorns, and Jeff got on the scoresheet on a 3-1 win.

Empty terraces at The Hawthorns, for the Reserve game against Forest in 1971

Back in the first team, it was not until November 13 that he recorded his first League goal of what was fast becoming a depressing season, in a 4-1 defeat at Nottingham Forest. By Christmas Howe had sold Kaye and Cumbes, and Albion were bottom of the First Division, having lost seven games on the trot. At the turn of the year Jeff was back in the Reserves, but as the first team started a recovery in January, Jeff won his place back in time for the home game with Manchester United on Saturday January 29. In front of the *BBC* TV cameras, and a crowd of 47,012, 'The King' helped the Baggies to a 2-1 win. Asa Hartford hit a free kick against the United bar and Jeff imperiously nodded in the rebound; then ran the whole length of the Rainbow Stand punching the air in delight.

By March, Jeff was back in the Stiffs again, scoring his last competitive goal of the season in a 2-1 home win over Aston Villa Reserves on March 28. His last glimpse first team action came at Molineux on April 15, when he sat out the game on the sub's bench as Albion won 1-0 to guarantee their First Division survival. He ended his worst-ever season in football with just two goals from his 22 appearances.

Don Howe reviewed the campaign soon after. "Astle had a hard season, what with an appendix operation and a knee injury. Jeff's strong point is his headwork in the box, but he has been one of our disappointments in that we have been unable to get the best out of him. Nevertheless, I am impressed by the way that Jeff has worked hard in training to overcome any set-backs. But each time he has looked like rediscovering form, he has suffered another injury. I can only sympathise with him like everybody else."

That knee injury turned out to be cartilage trouble, and in May Jeff went into hospital for an operation, which caused him to miss the

A classic Astle memory; his headed goal against Manchester United

club's pre-season tour of Sweden. This time Howe did not try to rush Astle back too soon. "There has been no attempt to force Jeff into a fast recovery. He has been given ample time to get himself right and was even able to enjoy a fortnight's holiday."

On his way back to fitness, Jeff played in a couple of second team friendlies, against Bath City and Aberystwyth, but it was not until August 23 that he played a 'proper' game, when he met up with his old team mate Clive Clark, as the Reserves beat Preston 1-0 at The Hawthorns. The knee was still giving problems, though, and it was back on to the treatment table before he was fit enough for another couple of outings with the Reserves by the end of September. "I feel better than at any stage of my recovery so far," was Jeff's verdict – just before his knee broke down once again. By mid-October, he was back in hospital for his second cartilage operation in five months. Howe sympathised. "This is a terrible blow for Jeff, who was working so hard to get fit. We all hope this latest operation will see an end to the injury problems that have dogged him for the past twelve months. He's a determined chap and he should be back in training within a month."

It was a depressing period for Jeff, who began pounding around the training track day in, day out. "I shall get back in the team. This enforced absence, in a way, has done me some good. It has revitalised my enthusiasm for the game and I am itching to get back into action. Never before in my career have I had such a bad injury spell; I seem to be having everything in one dose. But I have got lots of goal left in me."

It was December 15 1972 before Jeff was back in action, in a much publicised game for Albion's third team in an Midland Intermediate League game at Spring Road. Don Howe bet Jeff a pound that he would not score. Jeff took the wager and won – scoring twice in a 5-1 win against the Wolves kids, the second goal, a classic header from fifteen yards. Over five hundred fans packed the training ground for a match that usually attracted one man and his dog.

Although the game was a minor one, Jeff knew its importance to his career. "I reckon the goal I scored at Wembley in 1968 will always stand out as the goal of my career – but the two today were pretty important to me as well. I needed them badly to prove to myself that I've still got the scoring touch, despite the two month lay-off. It has also proved to me that the left knee would stand up to a match, although I must concentrate in strengthening the thigh muscles which have rested during my lay-off."

As ever, Jeff was quick to thank his fans. "After the game I was talking to a man from Worcester who said he had been up since 7 am so he could bring his two sons to come just to see me. I feel so very proud, because all the supporters have been so unbelievably good to me."

A handful of third team games followed, during which period Jeff was able to pass on some of his wealth of experience to the young Albion stars of the future, including future Albion coach John Trewick, and England star Bryan Robson – who was the apprentice professional responsible for cleaning Jeff's boots at that time. By January 1973, Jeff was marking time in the Reserves, as the first team once more slumped to the bottom of the First Division. On February 10 Jeff scored – and hit the woodwork – in a 3-0 win over Coventry. On February 24, Albion had a tough fifth round FA Cup tie at Elland Road, and Jeff was rushed back into first team action, but there was no fairy tale comeback as Albion went down 2-0. The following Wednesday marked Jeff's return to League action when Arsenal, top of the League, came to The Hawthorns. Jeff was inspirational. Although clearly lacking pace, he was able to outwit his young marker – Arsenal debutant centre-half Brendon Batson – to head down at the far post for Tony Brown to hit a late winner. Ten minutes from time Jeff left the pitch to a standing ovation from the adoring Hawthorns crowd.

Albion lost their next match in a crucial relegation battle – for both sides – at Old Trafford, but Jeff had the consolation of scoring his first League goal since January 1972 – coincidentally, also against Manchester United. "I've scored many memorable goals, but that one against United will always have a special meaning for me."

Those games were the start of a crusade to try to keep Albion in the First Division, where they had been for almost a quarter of a century. Jeff played in the last twelve games of the season, and scored another four goals, including the only goal in a 1-0 win against Leicester City, and goals in last two games against Manchester City and Birmingham. It was all to no avail; just when they seemed to have saved themselves, and despite Jeff's best efforts, Albion lost their last four games and were relegated to Division Two.

Laraine remembers how Jeff took relegation. "For all his laughing and joking, Jeff took his football career very seriously — obviously, because he would never have had the career, at the highest level that he did, otherwise. He took it very badly when Albion were relegated, very personally, and was determined that he would play his part in getting them back into the First Division. He knew what a challenge that that would be, though, especially under Don Howe; he always said that the Second Division was the hardest Division to get out of in the Football League."

On May 5 1973, with Albion relegated, Jeff elected to go into hospital again for an astonishing fourth cartilage operation – a dubious honour he reckoned he shared with another former Albion star, Joe Kennedy. It meant another gruelling fight for fitness – but while he was getting fit, he took his coaching certificate, and fitted in a couple of games of cricket for the Albion, at Edgbaston and Old Hill, as well as umpiring in a Benefit match for Warwickshire cricketer David Brown.

By the time the 1973-74 football season came round, Jeff was back in the third team – where he was joined by (his words) 'up and coming youngster' John Osborne, who had also fallen out with Don Howe, and was ready to quit the game prematurely.

The first team did not get off to the best of starts in the Second Division and Tony Brown was soon bemoaning the continued absence of his old strike partner. After a couple of good goals against Walsall's Youth side on October 13, Jeff played his first Reserve game of the season at Huddersfield three days later, nodding in a Barry Donaghy corner to register the second goal in a 2-0 win.

That was the start of a run of seventeen consecutive games for Jeff in the Central League – the longest spell in a Reserve side since his early days at County – and it was February 1974 before Howe gave him a chance in the first team.

On February 23 Albion played Bristol City at The Hawthorns, and Jeff made the senior side for the first time in nine months. When he trotted out before the game, his fans gave him a very special welcome, chanting "Astle is our King."

Ernie Hunt opened the scoring for City after a quarter of an hour. John Wile equalised five minutes later but Bristol scored again through Tainton ten minutes into the second half. In the 70th minute Albion levelled a second time – and it was the moment the crowd had been waiting for. Asa Hartford chipped a ball into the area onto the head of Astle, who nodded past Cashley, into the Birmingham Road goal.

It seemed as if Albion would re-launch their promotion challenge, as Jeff played in the next five games. At Bolton in a 1-1 draw he set up a goal for Tony Brown, but the following week they crashed 4-0 at home to Middlesbrough, and Jeff was dropped.

On March 30 Albion blew a two goal lead at home to Cardiff. In the second half, Jeff came off the bench to replace Tony Brown, for what turned out to be his last first team appearance for the club. Behind the scenes, the manager and the board were discussing his future. Notts County had come in with a £50,000 bid. The board had rejected the bid – but only to do Jeff a good turn. The season petered out with Jeff in the Reserves, and he played his last competitive game for the Albion in the Central League game at the City Ground Nottingham on April 27 1974, in a 1-0 defeat.

A few days later, when the club announced its retained list, Jeff was given a free transfer, and Howe explained his reasoning. "Ray Wilson and Jeff Astle are both due for testimonials next season. As Ray is first in the queue it would be unfair to the players and the public to have two testimonials running at the same time. For that reason we have decided to let Astle go on a free transfer in the hope that he can negotiate a good contract with whichever club he joins." That was why the Albion had turned down the £50,000 bid from Jeff's *alma mater* Notts County. Jeff subsequently spoke to Jack Dunnett, County's chairman, about re-joining his old club, but the pair could not agree terms regarding the size of Jeff's signing on fee, and the deal fell through.

On the last day of April, his last at the club he had served for a decade, Jeff went home as normal, walked into the house and told Laraine that he had been released. Just like that; no fuss, no bother. Laraine remembers well how low key Jeff's leave-taking was. "He just collected his boots, left early and came home. After all those years, how awful that was. And that was down to Don Howe – the camaraderie that used to be there had all gone."

Jeff spoke to the local press once it had sunk in. "It was a shock, even though I knew it was coming! I was told a week ago. It is good of the club to let me go on a free. I have enjoyed my ten years in West Bromwich, and we have made a lot of friends. I have seen many parts of the world I would not have had the remotest chance of seeing had I been an ordinary working chap. What I would like to do when I go, and wherever I go, is to take the Albion fans with me. So far as I am concerned, they have been the greatest. I shall never, never forget them."

Jeff would be sorely missed at the Albion – on the pitch, at the training ground on the team coach and in the dressing rooms. It had been in those settings that he had lightened the days and the long journeys with his infectious humour, a trait which never deserted him even in the worst hours of his two-year battle against injury. And even when he was leaving The Hawthorns for a new life away from the Albion, it was the fans who were first in his thoughts — which is why, to all Albion fans of a certain age, Jeff Astle will always be 'The King.'

The end of an era; Jeff's last Albion goal, v. Bristol City

114

Leaving The Hawthorns

In life, all good things must come to an end sometime. For Jeff, his glorious spell at the Albion had been spoiled in the latter years by the new managerial regime at the club, which perhaps made it easier for him to accept the inevitable. When his contract ended on the last day of the 1973-74 season, he quietly left the club that he loved so much.

But Jeff still had a few years football left in him. Less than a month later, he got a surprise phone call from Bobby Moore in South Africa. "Hello Jeff, I'm in Cape Town, playing for 'Budgie' Byrne's side, Hellenic – do you want to come out and play for us?" Although it would mean several weeks of separation for the Astles, the offer was too good to refuse, and Jeff never regretted his short spell of foreign football.

Jeff went in at the top – he made his Hellenic debut in the Final of the Coca Cola Shield Final against Maritzburg on Friday May 17, at Hellenic's Green Point ground, in front of 18,000 eager fans. The Maritzburg manager was none too pleased about having two World Cup stars suddenly playing against his team, and considered making an official protest about a side "buying" their way to a trophy. "The inclusion of Moore and Astle, two brilliant players, will make us even more determined." And it did; the first leg of the Final finished goalless.

Seven days later, excitement in Cape Town was still at fever pitch, as Hellenic took on their biggest rivals Cape Town City – managed by former Ipswich goalkeeper Roy Bailey – at City's Hartleyvale ground, where the home side had been unbeaten for two years. This time the attendance was over 25,000 for the Cape Town Derby, and again the result was goalless. Jeff was quoted in the *Cape Times*, "The standard of football is much higher than I expected."

On Tuesday May 28, Jeff was amongst the silverware again, although it was a close thing, in the second leg of the Coca Cola Shield against Maritzburg at the Jan Smuts Stadium. Hellenic were two goals down and seemingly out of it, but goals from Wilf De Bruin and, two minutes from time, from Andy McBride, salvaged a 2-2 draw – and Hellenic won the first trophy of the season, on the away goals rule.

Jeff was certainly back in the big time. His next game – his first in the South African National Football League — was against Johannesburg side Jewish Guild at the Rand Stadium, and the match attracted the biggest-ever attendance for a League game in South Africa, over 31,000 paying for admission. Partly that was down to the presence of Astle and Moore – but the real crowd-puller was George Best, fifteen pounds overweight, but as skillful as ever in the Guild side. Hellenic missed a penalty but grabbed a 1-1 draw with another goal from De Bruin.

The return game with Jewish Guild – who were managed by former Wolves star Mickey Lill – came on June 6, attracting another 20,000 crowd to Green Point. This time Best was upstaged by Jeff, who scored his first two goals for Hellenic in a 5-1 win that took them up from ninth to sixth in the table. Unfortunately, Jeff aggravated his old knee injury and missed the next game, another 0-0 draw against League leaders Arcadia Shepherds, in Pretoria. Jeff was back for the next match, a

The Cape Times, Friday, May 17, 1974

HELLENIC'S BIG THREE — Jeff Astle, manager Budgie Byrne and Bobby Moore. They are key figures in the Shield final against Maritzburg at Green Point tonight.

Too few grounds –Taylor

By Harold Butler

IAN TAYLOR, president of the Western Province Football Association has appealed to clubs to help alleviate the ground scarcity which is causing concern.

He told delegates at a special meeting on Wednesday that the scarcity of ground could seriously retard the expansion of soccer in the future and that unless the position improved clubs, especially those without a ground and those with a restricted use of their ground, could not expect to enter more teams in the competitions.

Taylor is particularly concerned about the high schools who have turned to soccer.

The association had fought for years to get the high schools interested. Now they had got it off the ground (there are 13 schools playing in three age groups) it would be a tragedy if progress is going to be hampered because of the lack of facilities.

Maritzburg fuming over Bobby Moore and Astle

Gloves off for the big game

By ANDRE VAN DER ZWAN

THE GLOVES are off. It's going to be a bare-knuckle fight when Maritzburg oppose Bobby Moore, Jeff Astle and nine other Hellenic faithfuls in the Coca-Cola Shield final (first leg) at Green Point tonight.

While 20 000 fans are expected to give Moore and Astle, two household names in British and world football, a rousing welcome, Maritzburg will most certainly not roll out the red carpet.

the idea, Jimmy Kerr, manager of Maritzburg, still feels the NFL should legislate that a club can only entertain one guest player a season.

Talking to Kerr in his

lenic party, we netted four more goals.

Kerr, like his Hellenic counterpart Johnny Byrne, is not naming his team till kick-off time. However, he indicated

DONALD GIE

Gie's knee is fine

By Harold Butler

DONALD GIE, Cape Town City left back, jarred a knee in a collision wit

116

6-3 home win over Durban City which took the side up to fourth. Four days later, on Tuesday June 18 an unchanged side beat Jewish Guild 3-1 in a Castle Cup tie, Jeff scoring the third goal with a delightful chip.

On Friday June 21, Bobby Moore played his last game for Hellenic, in a 2-0 win against struggling East London United at the BRU ground, before returning to England. He left them in a great position, in third place, just two points behind joint leaders Arcadia and Durban United, all three clubs having played 13 games. The next game was a 6-0 hammering of Boksburg in the League, and this time Jeff, now fully settled in, scored two and made two. Unfortunately, the Boksburg game was due to be Jeff's last before following Bobby Moore back home, but when Hellenic were drawn at home to top Mayfair side Rangers in the Castle Cup, Jeff readily agreed to postpone his departure by four days so he could play in one more game, on Friday June 28. What a shame that Jeff's unbeaten record in South Africa went west that day, Rangers winning 2-1 thanks to a last minute goal. Even so, it had been a successful six weeks, and Hellenic had moved from mid-table to a challenging position in the championship race whilst Jeff was with them.

"It was a fantastic country and Cape Town was a marvellous place," recalled Jeff afterwards, but the big drawback for Jeff, of course, was the flying – two and a half hours' flying time was typical for an away game in such a vast country.

There were darker themes as well. Jeff hated the apartheid system – he thought it was dreadful, and he could see the tension that was evident even in 1974. All the local-born white players in the Hellenic team had maids who lived in huts in the garden. Jeff could not adjust to that, nor to separate footpaths, restaurants, toilets and even water fountains for blacks and whites.

Jeff and Laraine got a first hand taste of how oppressive the white regime was. "In those days you had to book your international calls well in advance, and you had a long wait. Jeff booked a call from Cape Town, and right at the start of the conversation I was asking whether apartheid was as bad as everybody said – and there was a click and they cut us off! It's terrible when you think, to listen in to everybody's conversations, and censor the calls."

While Jeff had been away, Laraine had taken a call out of the blue, which would lead to the next, exciting phase of Jeff's career. "I took a phone call from Barry Fry, who we didn't know at that time, asking if Jeff could get in touch. I promised Barry that Jeff would ring when he got back from South Africa."

Back in England just before the start of the 1974-75 season, Jeff had had few concrete offers for the new campaign. Jimmy Sirrell, the manager of his first love, Notts County had approached the Albion, but Jeff could not come to a suitable arrangement with County chairman Jack Dunnett. From non-League there was Cheltenham Town who came in with an offer of a role as player-manager – something which Jeff did not relish. He had always said, "When I finish playing, that's it. I'm not going into management; there's too much back-stabbing." He duly got in touch with Fry, who had been appointed player manager at run-down Dunstable Town in March 1974.

The little Bedfordshire side were not a particularly attractive prospect, as Fry readily admitted. "My first two gates at the club were 34 and 43 people (My family came to the second game!) There was no football tradition in the town. Nobody knew Dunstable was there. When I asked George Best to come and play for me in a couple of games, he didn't know where Dunstable was. And when I told him it was near Luton, he didn't seem any the wiser then! Dunstable had done absolutely nothing; they had finished bottom of the Southern League for nine years running before I arrived."

Barry had his work cut out trying to convince Jeff to make the break with full-time football, but the persuasive character succeeded in the end. "Jeff Astle; the King. He has to be one of my best-ever signings. He'd just left the Baggies – who he loved, and loved till the day he died – because he'd just had had a cartilage operation. I spoke to him and

Jeff signs for Dunstable, with (l-r) Barry Fry, Keith Cheeseman, and Laraine

asked if he fancied playing part-time football. In the beginning, I don't think he did, really. But when he realised there were no offers coming in from League clubs, he wanted to play, because he really loved his football. So it enabled me to offer him a package to play part-time football with Dunstable. He used to train two nights a week in Dunstable, Tuesdays and Thursdays, and he did brilliant for us. "

The main reason for the startling upturn that was to change Dunstable Town for ever – and eventually lead to the club's destruction – was the arrival on the scene of a new chairman, Keith Cheeseman. The Midlands-based building magnate poured money into the near-bankrupt club, giving Fry a free hand – and the club just took off. Fry signed ten new quality players to transform a previously moribund side.

When he signed on July 22 1974, for Dunstable, bottom of the First Division (North), Jeff was by far the biggest star playing in the Southern League. To be able to pay him, Cheeseman offered him a job as a consultant with his building firm, W W Parrish, based in Rugeley, which provided Jeff with a salary and a company car, and enabled him to play for the club for just £25 a week.

Under Fry, Dunstable was clearly going places. He realised that he needed to raise the club's non-existent public profile. He knew he was competing with the likes of the up-and-coming Ron Atkinson, who had won the Southern League, down the road with Kettering. Using the cash – literally, for most of Cheeseman's finances involved large amounts of "readies" – that was now available, Fry bought George Cleary, Trevor Peck and John Hawksworth for £1,500 the three, from Kettering and Jackie Scurr and Jack Bannister – the former Albion defender, who had left The Hawthorns a few months before Jeff's arrival there in 1964 – from Cambridge United. It was easy signing quality non-League players – with the help of Cheeseman's cash, and the presence of a "name"

The Dunstable side that faced Cork Celtic, with Jeff (back row) and George Best

as big as Jeff Astle already at the club. Fry also tried – and failed – to sign Denis Law and Peter Bonetti.

But Barry Fry also had big ideas off the pitch as well. He, Jeff and Cheeseman travelled north to meet Manchester United manager Tommy Docherty and his assistant Paddy Crerand in a Manchester hotel before the pre-season games. Fry had once been one of United's Busby Babes – although he never made it to the first team – and had played for United Reserves alongside the likes of George Best. A £1,000 'bung' persuaded Docherty to send a United Reserve side down to Dunstable's Creasey Park. But Fry's real coup was to persuade his former Old Trafford team mate, George Best, to guest for Dunstable. Best had fallen out with Docherty, and was at the end of his United career, but he readily agreed to turn out for his old pal. The game attracted 10,000 people to the little ground, and was featured on News at Ten, as Dunstable beat a strong United team – with the likes of George Graham in the side — 3-2, after being two goals down at the break.

Another popular warm-up game followed, with George Best guesting again, against Bobby Tambling's Cork Celtic side, before the Southern League season started in earnest. Strangely enough, though, Jeff's Dunstable debut came on Saturday August 3, against a side he was VERY familiar with – the Albion Reserve team, Dunstable drawing 0-0 against a strong Baggies side containing the likes of Bryan Robson.

Not surprisingly, it took quite a while for the hastily put-together side to gel. Jeff made his Southern League debut on Saturday August 17, at Kidderminster's Aggborough stadium, and he had a quiet start – in fact, he was well shackled by the experienced home centre-half; former Albion team mate, Stan Jones! It took a last minute goal from another former Albion man, Jack Bannister, to earn Dunstable a point.

They lost their first home game of the season in disastrous fashion, 3-0 to eventual champions Bedford Town, and were soon eliminated from the League Cup by an average Corby Town side, Jeff scoring his first goal for the club in the 2-1 away defeat. Jeff's first goal in the League came in the return game at Bedford – a 1-1 draw – on September 9, and after that the goals really began to flow. He scored his first FA Cup goal for three years, the winner against Hertford in a first round qualifying match – this from the man who had scored the winning goal in a Wembley Cup Final! In 1968 there were 100,000 to cheer – this time there were only 183 people (and a dog) to see it...

Jeff played a major part in Dunstable's success that year, on and off the field, as Fry was the first to appreciate. "Without Jeff Astle we wouldn't have got promoted that year – no question. I'd seen Jeff play in the Reserves after returning from his cartilage operation. He wasn't as mobile as when I'd seen him in his heyday, but he still had that physical presence. And the goals he got! After Jeff signed, the gates climbed to over 1,000 a game, and we won promotion to the Premier Division, scoring 105 goals, which was unheard of, and that won us the Merit Award as top scorers in the Southern League. And Jeff got 34 of those goals."

Fry would also take Jeff's advice on signing players. "Yeah, Jeff was a good judge of a player. He was honest in his assessment. He's been with us a while before he started throwing in other names from the Albion Reserve side, like midfielder Stewart Woolgar. Roger Minton was a class full-back. Bruce Collard (brother of Jeff's Albion colleague Ian, and signed from Scunthorpe) was a hard, nasty bugger of a centre-half. He was a good judge of players and character as well; the three lads that I had on his say so from West Brom were not only good players, but good characters — good, honest pros."

Jeff certainly had something in common with Roger Minton – the youngster had fallen out with Don Howe! Why? He had refused to shave off his beard when the manager had insisted. At the time, a number of senior players – the likes of Asa Hartford – had grown beards to show their solidarity with Minton, but that show of independence signalled the end of what could have been a very good League career for the young full-back.

At heart, of course, Jeff was a professional footballer, pure and simple, and the job he had with W W Parrish was getting him down, as he made

Jeff in the unfamiliar all-white kit of Dunstable Town

clear to Fry. "After a couple of months Jeff just got fed up of driving around and looking at building sites and being the consultant – he just wanted to be in Dunstable, because he wanted to train all the time. He didn't want to train part-time, he missed the life of a full-time professional. He wanted to be in every day. So we devised a scheme where he trained every day, whilst becoming Dunstable's Commercial Manager. And he was brilliant at that, because he was like a magnet to people; everybody wanted to talk to him."

It was actually Jeff's idea. Because of his long association with the Albion, he came up with the plan of Dunstable selling the Albion's Lottery tickets. Dunstable couldn't lose on the deal. They got a commission on each ticket sold, Jeff got a commission, but if there was a big winner, the Albion, as the promoters, paid out, so Dunstable had no outlay at all. And it was Jeff who insisted on working on commission only. As Fry says, "He used to say 'If I don't earn it, I don't deserve it! – which was typical Jeff Astle. Who would say that nowadays? Players walk into your office and they expect ten grand just for standing there. Jeff did well. he made a lot – because he sold a hell of a lot of tickets."

To be able to do the job properly, Jeff had to move to the Dunstable area. Keith Cheeseman was in the process of moving to a new mansion in Houghton Regis, so he suggested that Jeff buy his old house at Clophill, to save him the hassle of looking for a new house. In fact, Cheeseman was in the process of writing Jeff a £10,000 cheque for his signing-on fee, and offered him the house – worth around £14,000, and including some high quality carpets and curtains – *in lieu* of a signing-on fee. It was a tempting offer, even when the deeds to the house were vaguely promised "soon."

Once he was living in the area, Jeff did a splendid job for the club off the field as well as on, as Fry readily acknowledges. "Socially, all the landlords of all the pubs and clubs around Dunstable, Bedford, Ampthill, Clophill and Luton knew him – everywhere he used to go with these lottery tickets, they used to love him. And there was nothing he wouldn't do for people – he was brilliant, and because of his attitude, our crowds just grew and grew. When you consider our crowds grew by three thousand percent – that wasn't just down to winning games. That was down to meeting people, promoting the club, doing a good job on the PR side. And that was all down to Jeff. They wanted to come and see Jeff, because he'd put himself out for them."

On the pitch, of course, Jeff was literally a marked man, as every part-time hoofer in the Southern League tried to make an impression on the former England man. "Without a doubt, everybody wanted to kick him, everybody wanted to take the piss out of him, but he was above that. He just got on with the game, and did the job, and scored loads of goals. All he would say is 'Don't worry Baz, I'll look after myself.' And he did! That's why he was so successful throughout his career."

The playing side, and the commercial activities were two sides of Jeff's influence at Dunstable, but there was a third – a facet of his career that he took to every club he played at – his dressing room bonhomie.

"He immediately won the respect of the other players at Dunstable, because of his application, his attitude and his professionalism. It was what he did for the team spirit. We'd be on the coach coming back from a defeat at Merthyr and he'd get all the lads going, playing cards, starting a sing-song – he always loved singing of course – and telling jokes. Before games, in the dressing room, he'd take the mickey out of all the lads, to get them to relax. The public never saw what he did in the dressing room. Some players are so petrified, even at non-League level, that they'll sit in the dressing room an hour before the kick off, not saying a word. They're all knotted up. But Jeff relaxed all that, with his attitude – but then once he got on the pitch he was the complete professional."

Three months into his new career at Dunstable, Jeff made a poignant return to his old stamping ground. The Albion had granted Jeff a Testimonial for his ten years' service to the club – but he could not have a full Testimonial Year because full-back Ray Wilson had already been allocated that benefit. Instead, Jeff's reward for a decade with the club was a one-off game, staged at The Hawthorns, on October 29 1974.

Had the match – between the current Albion side and the 1968 FA Cup-winning side – been staged a few years earlier, there would have been a full house to pay respect to the King. Even so, the attendance of 11,941 was only slightly less than the season's average for Second Division games.

And Barry Fry – like all the players and staff of Dunstable, was at the game that emotional evening. "We had two 52-seater coaches from Dunstable to go to that match. All the players and their wives went on the one coach, and a bus-load of supporters went on the other. And we all paid. Jeff offered us all complimentaries, but everybody paid to get in. And that match opened people's eyes. What he had that day – the crowd, and the raw emotion when he went on the microphone. My lads had never seen anything like the hero worship that they saw that night. And what really amazed them, was that somebody who was worshipped by so many people, and had a reason for being aloof — but wasn't! He was Jack the Lad, one of the lads. And that was why, throughout the Southern League, not just at Dunstable, Jeff got such respect, for his honesty professionalism as well as his ability to score goals."

Jeff and Laraine, who had made the arrangements for the game, were most concerned about the likely appearance of one of their guest players. They had managed to get the whole '68 side, with the exception of Clive Clark, who was unable to get down in time. In his place, Jeff had asked Barry to get George Best – but this was when nothing was certain about the Irish winger, and the Astle were worried about making promises to Albion fans, then letting them down.

When Jeff arrived at The Hawthorns to prepare for the game, the first question he asked the doorman was: "Has George Best arrived yet? Can you keep a special watch out for him, because I'm very worried that he won't turn up?" "It's OK, Jeff – he's been here and waiting for you for 25 minutes!" Not only had the wandering minstrel of football arrived – he had actually beaten both of his hosts, Jeff and Laraine, to the ground, by a considerable period of time! Of course, as Jeff noted at the time, even as a guest player at a Testimonial match in West Bromwich, George was surrounded by a coterie of "hangers-on" and self-appointed advisors who, in his opinion, were to prove the downfall of the player Jeff always described as "the best player I have played with or against, in the English game."

The Testimonial match was an emotional high-point which served as a fitting climax to a glorious career at The Hawthorns; and, in its way, also served as a "closure" for the thousands of Astle fans who had not really come to terms with the gradual slide out of the scene of their hero. This was definitely the last time that the fans would see Jeff in an Albion first team shirt, albeit actually playing against the current side, as part of an Albion '68 XI. And that was how Jeff actually preferred it.

Jeff in the familiar dressing room at The Hawthorns, with his 1968 team mates

He would rather be remembered, as a leaving statement, as it were, as part of that victorious and gloriously happy 1968 FA Cup winning side, rather than as part of Don Howe's dour, humourless and woefully unattractive side.

After the game, a small reception, hosted by Jeff and Laraine, was held in the players' lounge, but before that, Jeff fetched out a collection of cut-glass tankards that he had bought to present to all of the players who had taken part in the match, as a lasting souvenir of the occasion. Having handed out the tankards to his "own" side in the away dressing room, he walked across to the home dressing to give them out to the current Albion professionals. When he reached the locked dressing room door, he was warned off by the steward. "I wouldn't go in there if I were you, Jeff." And Jeff could hear why; behind the door, Don Howe was berating his players in pretty basic industrial language — for having lost a Testimonial game. Never let it be said that Howe approached friendly games unprepared; just as he had sent out a defensive team to grab a goalless draw in a Testimonial game at Bristol City in his first season at the Albion, he sent out this team with firm instructions that they were to play, at all costs, for a win. And that's what they did, to the extent that that Jeff's star player and crowd-puller, George Best, had to be substituted, for his own safety, after a number of agricultural tackles from Howe's hard man, Alan Merrick. It was some considerable time before the diatribe was completed; Howe stormed out, and Jeff, who had returned to the players' lounge to wait, was able to enter the dressing room and make his presentation.

By now, the Astles were living in Cainhoe Road, Clophill, and Jeff was applying himself to Dunstable full-time, as Fry well remembers. "Every morning when I was in at nine, Jeff was in at nine. Not to do his job, but to train. There were only two of us in; I would cross it and he'd bang the ball into the net. But he was such a dedicated bloke where football was concerned. If I would phone him at five past nine on a Friday night, Laraine would say, 'Barry, he's gone to bed and I daren't go in his room.' Friday night – it was religious; he went to bed early. Saturday and Sunday, 25 pints and all that on Sunday, you know what I mean! But he put some of today's players to shame with his professional attitude towards the game. Fantastic!"

And so many of Jeff's goals were had the mark of quality. "He scored so many great goals. Our keeper, Gary Steele kicked him a ball, got to be 70-80 yards, out of his hands, and Jeff ran and ran and it came over his head, and he hit it first time, into the net. It was something to even try to do that while you're running and the centre-half is pushing you. To even attempt to hit it. But Jeff hit the back of the net with it. What a goal – the place erupted. Another one was when our winger, Terry Mortimore ran 80 yards, beat everybody, then crossed, and Jeff, 18 yards from goal, climbed to head the ball and headed it harder than I can kick it. A fantastic goal. A terrific goalscorer. Jeff is the last great header of the ball I've seen. Who heads the ball nowadays? He was magnificent. And not just knocking them in with his head, but laying the ball off with his head, to his team mates. That's a dying skill. Nobody heads the ball any more. And he was so brave. Playing at my level, I'd see it coming and think, "Oh, pull out of that Jeff!" – but he wouldn't, he'd put his head in, and get kicked."

Fry's abiding memory of Jeff recalls a stormy incident in the dressing room. "We played Bedworth and we were 3-0 down at half time. I got all the lads in the dressing room. There was a knock on the door and a chap came in with a tray of cups of tea. Jeff said, 'OK mate, you'd better not come in here, give them to me' and he took them off him and shut the door. I said 'Cuppa tea? I'll give you a ***** cuppa tea!' And I kicked this tray – and all the scalding hot tea went all over Jeff. 'Get out, all of you; you don't deserve a ***** cuppa. You don't deserve a ****** half time break. Get out, all of you!' And they all ran out.

I just sat there for ten minutes before going out for the second half. And they scored five, we won 5-3, and Jeff scored a hat-trick. And when he scored the third he ran right over to me on the bench and stuck two fingers right in my face! But we went out together that night, and we had a good laugh about it. 'You really got my goat there Barry – I was covered in boiling hot tea and it hurt but I didn't want to show it was hurting.' A fantastic attitude that was typical of the man."

With Fry's brand of attacking football, results could be a bit "up-and-down." One week Dunstable would win 4-1 in the Southern League at Bromsgrove, the next they would lose 5-0 at Gainsborough in the Eastern Professional Floodlit League. But gradually, the side moved up the table, and really clicked over Christmas, scoring fourteen goals in two games, 6-2 at Bedworth and 8-1 at home to Witney, when Jeff recorded his first Dunstable hat-trick – unusually for Jeff, all with his right foot, rather than with his head.

In February Fry experimented with playing Jeff at centre-half in an EPFL game at Bexley. "I told Jeff it would extend his football career by at last three years if he would consider moving back in later seasons," explained Fry, but the *Dunstable Gazette* reporter commented on "the number of occasions that the side were caught out badly by Astle's slowness on the turn", and the experiment was not repeated.

At the end of Jeff's first season at Dunstable, promotion had been achieved in style. There was a bit of a hiccup at the end of the season, with a 2-1 home defeat by Bromsgrove – a game which reunited Jeff and his former Notts County team mate Tony Hateley. It was the latter's taunting of Bruce Collard that saw the youngster sent off, which decided the game. Seven days later, it seemed as if a 1-0 defeat at Banbury had cost Dunstable promotion, but wins over Wellington and, on the last day of the season, at Gloucester City, meant that Dunstable crept up above rivals Leamington, to clinch promotion.

Fry's exciting side were top scorers in all three divisions of the Southern League, thanks to the productive partnership between Jeff and George Cleary, and finished as runners-up behind Bedford Town, with 58 points, one point ahead of AP Leamington. And things were not much different in the Premier Division the following season; goals were not quite so easily to come by against the better sides of the standard of Wimbledon, Yeovil and Atherstone, but Dunstable stunned them all by heading the table for most of the season – until disaster struck. Jeff, unfortunately, would not be at Creasey Road for the start of the next season.

During the summer, Jeff was trying to sort out his new house at Clophill, but was having difficulty in getting hold of the chairman, to finalise the details, and after a while he asked Fry for advice. "Barry, I still haven't got the deeds to the house. What am I going to do?" Fry soon realised that he did not know everything about his chairman's financial activities. Perhaps he should have realised something when the £1,500 cheque that had been sent to Kettering for the three players, bounced. But there was worse – much worse – to come.

"Jeff found out that the property in Clophill had no fewer than 35 mortgages on it, that had never been paid. He didn't get the deeds because they were never Cheeseman's to give. There had been this 'second' mortgage and that 'second' mortgage. How the hell Cheeseman managed it I'll never know. By the time Jeff realised what had happened – when somebody knocked on the door to change the locks – he had really been stitched up; he had effectively paid £10,000 for a house that had mortgages worth £200,000 on it!"

For all his work at the club, Jeff was badly out of pocket thanks to a conman. The club was falling apart financially as well, and Fry was forced to sell all his best players – his forwards – to keep going. Southern League Premier side Weymouth made a £15,000 bid for Jeff, Fry's star asset, and the manager did the deal – but for just £5,000, to enable Jeff to get the best deal possible regarding wages and a signing on fee with the south coast club, although he in no way recouped the money he had been conned out of by Cheeseman. "Jeff was so upset, because he thought he'd bought a house, but he'd got nothing. I felt horrible, because I'd got him there, even though I didn't do the house deal. It was a terrible day for me, because I didn't lose him through football."

Fry and Cheeseman had an almighty row over Jeff, actually on the pitch at Dunstable. Cheesman, unaware that Fry had sold his star player, approached Fry, because Jeff had gone public about the chairman's dealings with the house. "This Astle.. he ain't doing this, he ain't doing that – he ain't doing **** all." "Keith. I've sold him." The two of them were face to face, and engaged in a blazing row. Fry was incandescent. "You don't ****ing treat my players like that. You better treat my players right, because if you **** them up like that, mate, I'm no longer with you. I've sold him, he's gone, and there's **** all you can do about it!" As Barry says now about the incident, "I thought Cheeseman would sack me, but he didn't. Mind you, if I had known then what I know about him now, I would have let him have done what he wanted!"

But Jeff's loss was a profound one to Dunstable, and Barry Fry. "I would have won the Premiership that year if we have kept the side the same. We were top with ten games to go, but I'd had to sell all my forwards. Jeff to Weymouth, Cleary to Cambridge, Terry Mortimore to Kettering, Lou Adams to Atherstone. We lost eight out of the last ten games 1-0, and finished 6th — then we got kicked out of the league, and demoted back to the First Division, all because of what Cheeseman had been up to."

And it was remarkable exactly what the Dunstable owner HAD been up to. In 1977 Cheeseman stood trial at Bedford Crown Court for having made bogus loan applications, using the names of the club's player, and others taken from the Peterborough phone-book, to a total of £300,000. The only Dunstable player whose name Cheesman did not use for a loan application was Jeff's – he was simply too well-known for that to have worked. Cheesman was jailed for six years. Soon after his release he was jailed at the Old Bailey for a further three years for blackmailing a bank manager into advancing him £38,000 and in 1992 he was arrested by Spanish police in Tenerife at the request of the FBI, who wanted him extradited on charges of laundering £292 million worth of stolen bonds – his involvement in the world's biggest-ever heist.

In the end, Jeff did well to get away from Dunstable when he did...

Weymouth, Atherstone, Hillingdon

Dietmar Bruck was the player-manager of Weymouth when Jeff left Dunstable and moved south at the start of the 1975-76 season. He was well aware of Jeff's power in the air from many torrid battles between his Coventry City side and the Albion, starting with the League Cup encounter between the two sides in 1965, when Jeff scored a brilliant hat-trick in a 6-1 demolition of Jimmy Hill's Sky Blues. It also helped Jeff that there was another name from the past – Bob Forrest, the former Notts County player – running a boarding house in Weymouth, a factor which undoubtedly helped him to settle in.

Jeff did not get off to the best of starts in his first game for the Terras, a friendly at Basingstoke on Saturday August 2 1975. It was not just Jeff who was making his debut – it was also Bruck's first game, whilst making his first appearance in goal for Weymouth was former Albion keeper Rick Sheppard. Weymouth lost 2-0, Sheppard dropped two clangers to gift the home side the goals – and Jeff was booked after a running argument with the referee!

Jeff's Southern League Premier debut came at Nuneaton on August 16, and although he was typically honest with his assessment of his performance afterwards – "I was not too happy with the way I played" – it was his goalbound header which was handled on the line by Nuneaton defender Kirk Stephens in the last minute, the resulting penalty earning Weymouth a 1-1 draw.

A week later, Jeff scored his first goal for the Terras in a 2-0 home win over Margate, and went on to score another thirty goals, finishing as top goalscorer for the south coast outfit. Weymouth, although they were financially sound, were no Dunstable on the pitch, and finished that season in 17th place in the Premier League. A playing colleague at the time at Weymouth was Graham Carr – later to manage, amongst several other clubs, Weymouth, Blackpool and Northampton Town – and he remembers the effect Jeff had on the other players at the Recreation Ground. "Jeff just loved playing the game. He had so much enthusiasm for playing, and he was a real star at Weymouth. He was one of the top players in the Southern League – not just with the fans, but in the dressing room as well. The players there looked up to him so much, because of what he had done with Albion, and with England. And he was such a lovely fellow as well."

Realising that he was coming close to the end of his playing career, Jeff took the opportunity to sow the seeds for his subsequent career once his time in professional football was at an end. As always, as at the Albion and Dunstable, Jeff was the life and soul of the dressing room at Weymouth, and worth his place in any side for the effect he had on both relaxing and lifting the spirits of his playing colleagues. One hot summer's day he was on the beach talking with Graham Carr. He had built up a window-cleaning round to earn some extra cash to supplement what he earned from football, and Jeff was interested, as Graham recalls. "There wasn't a lot to do around Weymouth – not much work, because there was no industry or anything there. Jeff used to come along with me on the window-cleaning round, just to give me some company, and he decided to take it up as well. I can remember him up the ladders, and a catch-phrase of his was 'If only Tony Brown could see me now!'"

Jeff soon bought his own ladders, fixed a rack on the roof of the family car, and took the first steps on a path that was later to lead to the establishment of his own industrial cleaning business. The amount he earned was not that great – no more than £20 a week to add to his football income – but as he said at the time, "I might as well as be doing something useful, rather than lying on the beach in my spare time. Being a famous footballer doesn't pay the bills. You can't live on that for the rest of your life."

In fact, the window cleaning began to occupy more and more of his spare time; he would work a few mornings a week, relax and play with the children on the beach in the afternoons, and then train with Weymouth – and his part-time colleagues – in the evenings.

Surprisingly, considering the injury problems he had had in his last three years at the Albion, Jeff's career, once he left The Hawthorns, was pleasingly free of injury. His arthritis would continue to cause him considerable discomfort, but he missed precious few games during his time at Dunstable, Weymouth and, later, Atherstone. Jeff even reckoned that his window-cleaning helped to extend his playing career that little bit more – "The climbing up and down ladders all day helped keep my knees supple!"

Jeff in the stripes of Weymouth

Jeff and Laraine – and their daughters Dorice and Dawn — lived on the sea front at Weymouth, in what had once been municipal offices of some sort, but which had been converted into flats, and bought by the football club, so that they could provide accommodation for any new signings.

Laraine has fond memories of the Astle's stay at the seaside. "We lived in the basement flat, so that we had our own entrance, with a yard at the back, which was handy because we'd got a dog at this point." Living in the ground floor flat was Dick Shepherd, and above him was the manager, Dietmar Bruck (with whose wife Maureen, Laraine was soon to forge a close friendship), whilst later residing in the second floor flat was Graham Carr.

Jeff moved his family moved down to Weymouth in February 1976, and were able to enjoy the fabled summer of 1976. As Dawn, then a lively eight year old can remember fondly, she used to spend a lot of time with her father on the beach, both during that long hot summer and after training at the club. "We used to go crabbing with Dad on the beach. I'd pick up these massive crabs – I wouldn't dare touch them today — and place them on Dad's sun-lounger when he was asleep. A big crowd would gather above us on the promenade, and you could hear them laughing as these crabs would gradually crawl up Dad and wake him up. He'd chase me for ages, and then duck me in the sea!"

Jeff would also get involved when young Dawn and Dorice – now both long-serving police officers – received an instant ban from the local amusement arcade for "fiddling" the roulette and horse-racing machines. Several times the two kids would storm across the road back to their flat demanding that their father intervene and use his celebrity to reinstate them at the arcade – and it usually worked!

Jeff's sojourn at Weymouth was fairly brief, but it won him many more friends. On January 24 1976, for the only time in his professional career, he had an undisputed four goal haul — all of the goals in Weymouth's 4-1 home game against Cambridge City, whose manager Roy Johnson observed afterwards, "Jeff Astle was superb. He's still in a class of his own in the Southern League — and he's a good half of the Weymouth team!"

At the end of January, Jeff had to go into hospital for some manipulation on a painful back. The treatment involved five visits to the outpatients department in a week, and he was supposed to be fit for the Saturday game, but the pain persisted and was out of the side until March 10. While he was away, the side went eleven games without a win without their top scorer, and dropped towards the relegation zone. When he returned he scored his 31st — and last — goal of the season against

Nuneaton, and he remained in the side as it struggled as high as 17th place. So bad were Weymouth that Dietmar Bruck retained just seven of the squad at the end of the season.

The following year was a disaster; Weymouth went straight to the bottom of the table and Jeff, in dispute with the club over a £2,000 payment that he had been promised, did not play well. He scored just one goal in his ten games — and that was his last goal for the Terras, coming in the 1-0 cup replay win against Waterlooville. His last game was on October 11, in a 2-1 win at Gravesend, and by then the side was making a recovery, inspired by the signing of one of Jeff's former colleagues. Aniello Iannone, who Jeff persuaded to move from Dunstable. The youngster went on to give Weymouth ten years excellent service, and later Ron Atkinson took his Albion side to Weymouth to play in his Testimonial game.

By then, after being dropped for Weymouth's 5-1 defeat at Kettering, Jeff realised it was time to move on, when Atherstone came in with an offer. "I enjoyed every second of last season, but this year it has gone a bit sour. I have just not been happy, and that has shown in my performances."

Jeff signed for Atherstone in October 1976. They had been the surprise package of the previous season, finishing third in the Premier Southern League Premier Division and winning the Birmingham Senior Cup. Barry Fry – he had moved on to Bedford Town after Dunstable's collapse — remembers getting a phone call from Gil Merrick, the former Birmingham City and England goalkeeper, who was then manager of Atherstone. Fry was quick to recommend Jeff. "If he's coming back to the Midlands, you've got to take him, because he's absolutely different class in the dressing room as well as on the pitch. He always takes it serious, and he's a great clubman. I saw Gil at an old players' do, years later, when I was manager at Blues, and he said to me 'You were right about Jeff – top man!'" Merrick paid £2,000 to Weymouth to get his man; already at Atherstone were his former Dunstable and Albion team mates Roger Minton and Bruce Collard.

Atherstone were struggling that season, and Jeff suffered a horrendous start at Sheepey Lane. His debut came at Gravesend on Saturday October 23 1976, and Jeff had a quiet game in a 2-0 defeat, which kept the Adders bottom of the League. In the next game, at Grantham the following Wednesday, Bruce Collard tore his cartilage after ten minutes, and was rushed to Grantham Hospital. Twenty minutes later, with Atherstone two goals down, Jeff joined him, when he broke two ribs in a sickening collision with Grantham keeper Chris Gardiner. Collard had to have an operation that kept him out for the rest of the season. Jeff was detained for four days – but, amazingly, ten man Atherstone came back to win the game 3-2!

That nasty injury sidelined Jeff for two months, and it was not until Boxing Day that he made his long awaited home debut for his new club, in a 2-1 defeat by Kettering which anchored the Adders firmly to the bottom of the table. Two days later Gil Merrick, his coach Reg Brassington and reserve team boss Les Dolphin were all sacked, and Joe Kiernan was appointed caretaker player-manager, with former Birmingham City star Malcolm Beard – who was in a contractual dispute with the club, and had issued a writ against them — as his assistant.

Jeff, still not match-fit, kept his place in the team under the new management team, and scored his first goal in Atherstone colours in a 1-1 draw with Cheltenham Town in the FA Trophy. In the replay at Whaddon Road, Jeff scored again, a magnificent header in the 20th minute of extra time, the only goal of the game, and only Atherstone's fifth win of a dreadful campaign.

Jeff, with just two goals under his belt by February, soon felt the effects of the change of management. In February, he linked up once more with Barry Fry, who had been appointed the new manager of Hillingdon Borough on the very day that Jeff had been holed up in Grantham Hospital. He approached Kiernan to take Jeff on loan at the mid-table Premier side, taking him for a month to pair him up once more with George Cleary – renewing a partnership that was responsible for over seventy goals between them in one season at Dunstable. "I'm very pleased with my capture," crowed Fry as he left the home of Atherstone Secretary Keith Allen. But the move was not a success. Jeff played his first game for Hillingdon in a 1-0 defeat at Dover on Wednesday February 9. Three days later, he played again in a 2-0 defeat at Telford's Buck's Head ground, where he aggravated his bad knee once again, and did not play again for the club before returning to Atherstone.

On Tuesday March 15 Kiernan was given the manager's job at Atherstone in his own right, and his side celebrated with a 2-1 win over the West Midland Police side. On the bench were Roger Minton and Jeff Astle, in his first game back at the club. Jeff was on the bench again for the 3-0 home defeat by Minehead, but was back in the side in time for the visit of Barry Fry's Hillingdon. Barry Fry wisely put two centre-halves onto Jeff in that game, and the visitors won 1-0. He had more luck against another former club, Weymouth, who were the only side between Atherstone and the bottom of the table; he won the penalty which, when converted by a young Malcolm Shotton, was the only goal of a crucial game. That 1-0 win over the Terras signalled a change in the club's fortunes, for results improved dramatically towards the end of the season.

There was an interesting clash on April 27, when Atherstone played hosts to Telford – the two rival centre forwards were two men who once had battled for possession of the England number nine shirt – Jeff Astle and Geoff Hurst. Although the game finished 0-0, according to all the reports, Jeff still looked the better player. On April 30 Jeff scored one goal and made another in a 3-0 home win against Maidstone. That was a goal to cherish, for it was the last one that Jeff would score in competitive football.

Characteristically, Jeff was collecting silverware right up to the end of his career. A good unbeaten run not only ensured that Atherstone would avoid relegation, it also took them to two local cup finals.

On Monday May 23 Jeff played on the big stage in a competitive game for the last time, as Atherstone took on Redditch in the Birmingham Senior Cup Final at St. Andrews. Although Atherstone's former Villa goalkeeper, Colin Withers had a brilliant game, he was beaten three times in the second period of extra time, as Redditch triumphed 3-0. But Jeff ended with a winner's medal in his very last game, two days later. He played in his side's 1-1 draw against Burton Albion at Eton Park, in the first leg of the Midland Floodlit Cup Final, collecting his medal two days later, albeit from the bench, as a non-playing substitute, as Atherstone won the second leg of the Final 2-0 at Sheepey Lane.

Jeff could have continued in non-League football the following season,

Jeff (centre, back row) lines up at Stoke in May 1997 — sharing the pitch with several other well known names from Albion's past, including Cyrille Regis, John Wile, Derek Statham, Steve Lynex and Kevin Summerfield

and even played for the Albion – for Burton Albion came in for him when they heard he was being released by Atherstone – but Jeff knew that at some stage, he would have to make the decision to quit the game that he had played, and loved, for more than eighteen years, and this was the time that he decided to make the move.

He had established his family in the lovely village of Netherseal, near Burton on Trent, and, after advertising his window cleaning services in the Burton newspapers, had been inundated with work, so he sat down with Laraine to discuss the future. He knew, at 35, even with his arthritis, he could perhaps carry on playing non-League football for a few years more, but increasingly, his major income would have to come from the cleaning business, and with so much work available, he decided to make a clean break, and retire from the game. As Laraine says, "A decision had to be made to pay the bills for the next twenty years, and Jeff decided that, at his age, football could no longer be relied on."

Jeff rarely played the game again after that; it was a very special occasion when he pulled on a shirt for an Albion Old Stars' team, but many supporters will remember two such treats. One was in a warm-up game for the John Wile Testimonial in 1981 – when he was disappointed because he had the chance to score a "final goal" in front of his beloved Brummie Road End, but topped his shot from the penalty spot.

The last time that Albion fans saw Jeff play in public, on a League ground, was in a similar game, as a warm-up for the League match between Stoke City and West Bromwich Albion in the First Division on May 4 1997 – the last League match ever to be played at the Victoria Ground.

That game – he got a tremendous reception from the fans of both Stoke and the Albion, and was in no way upstaged by another "great," Sir Stanley Matthews – was Jeff's last appearance in the spotlight, at least as far as playing football was concerned. He settled down to a more mundane, but equally enjoyable life with his cleaning business, able to devote even more time to his family. His youngest daughter, Clare, had been born in November 1978, and by now, Dorice and Dawn had made Jeff a devoted grandfather as well.

In later years Dawn used to accompany her father on many of his jobs – in his company van, with "Jeff Astle never misses the corners" printed on the side. "We would be up at 5.30, grab a bacon and egg sandwich – and then be off to cleaning toilets after the Donnington Rock concerts. I did the women's toilets. You needed a strong stomach – it was absolutely vile! Unblocking toilets with a plunger and long rubber gloves on – which once, overflowed all down the inside of Dad's gloves. But he just used to laugh it off. He used to give me a penny per black bag that I filled with litter –

and then asked me to try to recruit my mates from school! It was a hard job, but he never said 'I'm Jeff Astle, I shouldn't be doing this.' He never asked anybody for anything, and he worked for the whole of his life after football."

Jeff loved village life, but always sought solace at home, where he could always relax from football. He very rarely spoke about his former career in the game, unless, as happened so often, he was approached by one of his many fans, and he was pleased to chat. He cleaned a factory in Burton for many, many years – at least fifteen years — but it was only after Jeff died, and they saw his photograph in the national dailies, that they even realised that the man who cleaned the factory was a former Albion and England superstar.

Jeff was also able to devote more time to his many sporting interests. He returned to his first love, cricket, playing first for Netherseal St Peters and then Netherseal Colliery. He was a really good all-rounder, who was usually top scorer for whatever side he played for, but in particular he was a brilliant catcher. When, later on, he was captain of Old Netherseal, and they were short, he would co-opt Dawn, who was there officially as scorer, and place her, dressed in boots two sizes too large and her Dad's cricket jumper, as a extra "man."

Jeff liked most sports, except golf, and played several well. He particularly liked pool, and won a beautifully carved pool cue in the Burton League. Dawn was usually tagging along. "When we used to go together to Albion away games, in the nineties, we would go for something to eat in a pub before the match, and we would have to search round for a pub that had a pool table. We went in some right dives to get a game of pool, I can tell you! Dad taught me how to play, and even then, he used to press on me, 'You get nowt for coming second.' "

Once a betting man, always a betting man. Jeff loved the greyhounds, and used to go to Perry Barr on Tuesdays and Monmore Green on Thursdays. When he took Dawn, whichever of them had won at the end of the night, would treat the other to an Indian or a Chinese takeaway on the way home. "I remember Dad always wanted what you had, because he always thought it was better than what he's had. He'd order something himself which turned out to be horrible, then kept on all the way through the meal trying to take mine!"

Eventually, in 1995, he bought his own greyhound, Skippy, which won a lot of races. Breeder Peter Billingham (the former Albion player) kept the dog at his kennels at Wombourne. Skippy was black with a touch of white on his paw and on his underside. Laraine remembers that, much as he loved the dog – Jeff always loved a winner — he had problems with him. "He had been bred by a women breeder. If Jeff got the lead he would panic and tie Jeff up in the lead, round his legs, so Jeff could never hold the lead and take him for a walk, so I had to walk him. But he won lots of trophies, and a lot of money. A lot of people would bet on Skippy purely because he was Jeff's. But he was a fast finisher. Once he got his nose in front, he was a great stayer, and would always win. We had him as a three-year old, until he got a bad foot injury, from which he never really recovered."

Best of all, for Jeff, was horse-racing in general, and the Cheltenham Festival in particular, and every March Laraine would lose him for a week, from Monday to Thursday "When it came around, he was like a little kid; he loved it so much, and looked forward to see it so much. He used to go with Tony Brown when he was at the Albion, but, of course couldn't stop the week then, because of training, so then he just went on Gold Cup Day. In later years he went with his mate Dennis Minns and they always stopped at the Royal Hop Pole in Tewkesbury, and they went from pub to pub playing dominoes, meeting old friends. He knew Terry Biddlecombe – Bill Beaumont and Josh Gifford both used to stay at Biddlecome's house, and Jeff used to go round to visit them when he was there. For Jeff, Cheltenham was what National Hunt racing was about. He had no interest in Ascot or the Grand National. And he was happy whether he won or he lost – but he usually won!"

Jeff's connections with the Albion were still very strong. In 1986, the club launched its Bond Scheme, based on a system that Bolton Wanderers had run very successfully, and the Albion cashed in on Jeff's popularity with the fans to promote the scheme. He was also President of the official Albion Supporters Club, and frequently appeared at club functions, driving all over the Midlands to entertain the fans, and reminisce about the great times at The Hawthorns. He was a regular visitor to the ground of course, following the team through thick – and mostly – thin – through the eighties and nineties.

He remembered being in a pub outside Highbury before the FA Cup semi-final against Ipswich in 1978. He couldn't believe his eyes when he watched the *BBC's Football Focus* – and saw Ron Atkinson being interviewed, with the FA Cup, at Wembley. "There is nothing that spurs on the opposition more than you being so cocksure. I just could not believe that Ron Atkinson could go out at Wembley with the FA Cup. It was like giving Ipswich a two goal start, if they were sitting there watching it." They were – and strong favourites Albion lost 3-1 to Bobby Robson's men, who went on to collect the Cup themselves at Wembley.

Those were the good times. In later years, as Albion declined, Jeff would regularly be called on assist on commentaries and to do media work – he had a regular column in the *Sports Argus* — and comment on the club's plight as they dropped, unthinkably, into Division Three. But he never criticised the club. "We've got the fans, we've got the ground, we've got the set-up – we should be in the Premier League." What he meant, of course, and admitted in private, was: "The club should be up there, but the players just aren't good enough at the moment." He felt particularly sorry for Paul Williams, who came in for "donkey" chants from his own fans soon after signing from Stockport in 1991. Jeff would seek him out after the game, and have a chat. "Unlucky, but keep trying – it'll come" to try to boost his confidence.

Jeff was stunned when the club finally dropped through the trapdoor into Division Three. He travelled all round the country to watch them, and could believe some of the grounds his beloved Albion were playing at. Dawn, who was – and still is — a regular away traveller, recalls, "It really upset him to see them at the likes of Mansfield, Twerton Park and Hartlepool." Or The Shay. He was a summariser for Sky, who were covering the match live when Albion played Halifax Town in the first round of the FA Cup in 1993, and was asked for his comments when Albion went down 2-1 – the first time that they had been eliminated at such a stage for nearly a century. "If I really say what I want to say, we shall go off air…"

In 1993 Jeff was co-opted onto the club's Public Relations Committee, which regularly met at West Bromwich Town Hall – the big man was a one-man Albion PR Committee, all by himself – even though he was very much dissatisfied with the way that the club was being run at that time, and he had a number of public disagreements with then chairman Trevor Summers. It was one such "bother" that ended Laraine's trips to The Hawthorns with Jeff, after nearly thirty years of faithfully watching the club.

Jeff carried on supporting, and was there at Wembley – a big outing for the whole family when the Albion beat Port Vale in the Play-off Final. For home games it could be a struggle to actually get to the match at times. Dozens of fans would stop him on the way from the car park, just to talk about the Baggies. It could take him twenty minutes to cross Halfords Lane, and it was always a rush to get to his seat on time. But, as Laraine remembers, he would always stop to talk. "He would always chat, he would NEVER refuse to sign his autograph, all through his career. It was a love affair with the Albion fans. I don't think any other Albion player has ever had that sort of relationship with the supporters – and probably never will again."

Fantasy Football

There's no doubt about it; like many of us, Jeff had always had a hankering to be a pop star. And, on a couple of occasions, he was. Back in 1970, before the World Cup in Mexico, Bill Martin and Phil Coulter, pop songwriters magnates responsible for Sandie Shaw's Eurovision winner, Puppet on a String, wrote Back Home, sung by the World Cup squad, and starring one Jeff Astle. As a former church chorister whilst at school, Jeff was the best singer of the 22, by quite some margin. And he was keen, as Laraine recalls. "Jeff loved everything about the Back Home single and LP. In the studio, they put him right at the front, by the microphones, and put the 'grunters' – Jack Charlton and Nobby Stiles and ones who just couldn't sing – at the back, so you can hear Jeff's voice clearly right up front in the mix on several of the songs on the LP."

The single reached number one in the charts in April 1970, remaining there for three weeks before being knocked off the top by Mungo Jerry's In the Summertime, and Jeff made a much-envied appearance on Top of the Pops. (not his first TV appearance of course – he'd been

Jeff, front row, singing 'Back Home' and soaking up the TOTP atmosphere

appearing regularly on *Match of The Day* and *Star Soccer* for years!)
The single actually lasted longer than the World Cup itself; the England squad were long "back home" from Mexico themselves when the single slipped out of the chart after sixteen weeks.

Naturally, after the South American "tour", "the band" released an album – Back Home, issued in a now rare and very expensive circular football cover, and containing renditions of the likes of: Lily The Pink, Sugar Sugar, Congratulations, There'll Always be an England and – of course – Puppet in a String. So, number one at The Hawthorns, Number one in the pop charts. It was a great start to Jeff's professional singing career.

Twelve months later, as is usually the case with a with all great pop artists, Jeff went solo. He got together with Carl Wayne, the Birmingham-based singer from the Move (and his wife, "Miss Diane" from Crossroads) to release his own single, Sweet Water.

"It was all Carl's idea," recalls Laraine Astle. "We went with Carl behind the scenes to see them recording an episode of *Crossroads*, featuring his wife, of course, and then Jeff recorded the single, Sweet Water, which Carl wrote for him." The single (backed with a Carl Wayne piano instrumental) was released on RCA Victor, and sold well. Once again, Jeff was at number one – but not on Top of The Pops this time.

In those days, the West Bromwich–based record shop Turner's (in old Paradise Street) issued its own "local" chart, published weekly in the *West Bromwich Chronicle* – and Jeff sold a steady stream of singles, at 50p each, that took him to the top of the local chart. He was autographing those singles for years afterwards.

That best-selling England album, with Sweet Water as a bonus track, was re-released on CD (Retro 805) in August 1995, to mark Jeff's return to singing – once again in front of millions on national TV. How did it happen? Jeff told the story on the liner notes of his CD.. "Frank Skinner is a West Brom fanatic and he idolised me when I was a lad. One day he rang me up and asked if I'd like to go on the his TV programme. So I went down to the studios in London, and everyone there really welcomed me." That first appearance on Fantasy Football was a real "one-off".

It was as a star of the 'Phoenix in the Flames' section of the show, in the first series, in 1994, when Baddiel and Skinner re-enacted great moments from football history. Rather than choose the obvious — Jeff's 1968 FA Cup winner, or, heaven forbid, his Brazil miss — Frank went for his controversial "offside" goal against Leeds, in 1971. And as Frank quickly recognised, "Jeff was a natural. As well as being a nice bloke, he had genuine comic timing and was incredibly keen to help, as was shown when he uttered a phrase that went straight into *Fantasy Football* folklore, 'My wife'll be Gary Sprake.'"

With Jeff playing himself, of course, and Frank and David Baddiel taking on the roles of Colin Suggett and Tony Brown, the watching millions were given a less-than-instant replay of the goal that turned the 1970-71 League championship.

It was the start of a beautiful friendship, as everyone who saw Frank's tear-stained face at the Albion-Walsall game in 2002 will testify. Frank soon got Jeff back on the show on a more permanent basis.

"I went down again at the start of the next series and Frank threw a piece of paper at me and said "This is what you're singing! I hadn't a clue that I was meant to be doing it, but the song (Love Grows Where My Rosemary Grows) seemed to go down well, and then they asked me back. They often gave me a really big build-up, which is nice."

Frank had neglected to tell Jeff exactly what his role would be, and Jeff and Laraine travelled down to Capital Studios Wandsworth thinking that Jeff was being invited for a one-off appearance as one of the guest "managers," and it was not until rehearsal time that Frank explained Jeff's new starring part in the show.

Delia Smith was one of the first *Fantasy Football* managers in new series, so, looking for a culinary link (however dubious) for the song, the producers chose *Love Grows (Where my Rosemary Goes)*, which Jeff performed to perfection, with Skinner and Baddiel in the

Jeff, Frank Skinner, David Baddiel and 'Statto' — the Fantasy Football regulars

background waving sprigs of rosemary.

Why Jeff? Frank had been one of those many fans of his who, back in 1971, had bought a copy of *Sweet Water*. He remembered that, and decided to launch a new section of the show, "Jeff Astle Sings."

In the first few programmes, Jeff used to sing in casual dress, but as the series progressed, he would be dressed in more and more elaborate outfits – the Statue of Liberty, Madonna, an Albion throstle, Ziggy Stardust – and his reception from the studio audience would become more and more riotous. Perhaps his oddest moment was his duet with his wife – when the producers had him dressed in an identical outfit to Laraine!

If only; Jeff cradles the World Cup in the Fantasy Football studio

Not surprisingly, she remembers the occasion well. "It was the Weather Girls' song, It's Raining Men, and Jeff had never heard of it – and neither had I. I think we were the only two people in the studio who had never heard of the song, and it took a lot of effort, and a lot of help from the studio staff, for us to learn the song in time."

In the early days of Jeff's new-found – or rather, bearing in mind his Top of The Pops appearances, his revived — singing career, the producers of *Fantasy Football* seemed to delight in dreaming up the most obscure and difficult songs for Jeff to sing, especially bearing in mind that he was only told of the selection on the morning of the recording of the programme, leaving him just a few hours to learn the song and the arrangement. Jeff's musical tastes inclined towards Neil Diamond, the Beach Boys, and the like, and it could be very bizarre to see and hear him singing Madonna's Like a Virgin, and, worst of all, Michael Jackson's Earthsong. Later on, the producers asked Jeff to submit a list of songs that he liked, and that he was familiar with, and, in the main, they stuck to the list.

There could be problems, though, especially when Jeff was unable to hear the backing tape over the noise of the audience, so it was fortunate that Laraine was on hand offstage to key Jeff in – a function that became a permanent fixture of the show from there on, and watching the tapes of the show now, it is possible sometimes to see Laraine (equipped in later shows with floor manager's headphones) standing by the autocue almost conducting the music and signalling to Jeff at the start of each new verse.

Jeff was soon a fixture on the programme. In the week that Eric Cantona spoke of "the seagulls following the trawler" Jeff came on dressed as a trawler, and Dave and Frank danced behind him holding up photos of Steven Seagal. When Jeff's next door neighbour from his Eastwood childhood, wrote to Frank describing how she used to scrub his back when he was a baby, Frank had Jeff wheeled in at the end of the show in a tin bath – with his former neighbour scrubbing his back, whilst he sang 'There's no business like show business! Jeff – and Frank – loved it all. "Jeff was a real pro. At heart he was a showman. He had milked the applause as an Albion player, and he loved showing off on the telly." And why not?

With the shows attracting over three and a half million viewers – a ratings record for its late time slot — Jeff appeared on dozens of shows, over the three series that ran to 1996. In 1998, the show had a big money transfer from BBC2 to ITV, and was broadcast live four times a week during the World Cup coverage from France, with ratings topping six and half million.

Very few shows now go out live on national television, and as Laraine recalls, it could be a hair-raising experience. "You could see it in Frank and David's faces. You could see and feel the tension. And you were at the mercy of the guests. Sylvia Kristel had no sense of humour at all. Then there was Bridget Neilsen, who was very much the worse for drink. And Johnny Rotten, from the Sex Pistols. Frank said that on that show he had either side of him his two heroes, Jeff and, from his Punk days, John Lydon."

Anyone who saw Rotten on the infamous Bill Grundy show back in 1977 might have worried what he might be like again on a live show, and Laraine and Jeff were to discover that the ageing Sex Pistol still had a taste for the outrageous. "Because of his antics on the set – flicking lit cigarettes into the audience and pushing a member of the crew into a bookcase — we ended up getting locked out of the studio when Jeff was due to come in and sing the closing song, while the floor manager was tidying up the mess and stuffing Lydon into a taxi to get him off the premises!"

Almost by accident, Jeff decided to exploit his renewed moment of fame, and moved out on his own into show business. "A friend of mine had organised this big do at Nottingham University, and he asked me if I would go along and do a song. I got there at 2 am and the place was packed. I was

There really was only one King — and it wasn't Elvis! Jeff on the road

144

more nervous than I had ever been in my life. I did Agadoo and the place went mad and wouldn't let me get off. So I did a few more – Back Home, Without You, Sailing, Travelling Light, Hi Ho Silver Lining. I got home at about 4 am."

That was the start of "Jeff's Roadshow," which toured universities, colleges and local clubs, including, on a number of occasions, the Albion's own Supporters Club, as well as their annual *Player of The Year* evening – with great success.

Memorably, in April 1997, Jeff was invited by Sheffield United, to regale their supporters, before their game with the Albion at Bramall Lane, with a rendition of the Blades supporters' 'signature tune,' based on John Denver's Annie's Song, but with lyrics adapted along the lines of: "You lift me... like a packet of woodbines," and so on. And what a great response it got from the home fans. But Jeff being Jeff, he couldn't just leave it at that. "I'm not just singing this. I've got Albion fans over there as well!" So he sang "And it's West Bromwich Albion, West Bromwich Albion F.C. They're by far the greatest team, the world

Jeff wows both sets of fans at Bramall Lane in 1997

has ever seen" — and made sure his REAL public following did not go away disappointed.

Jeff's last appearance as a TV star came on *Fantasy Football* in 1998; as usual, he closed the show, and the series, with a song, poignantly, "We'll meet again." With that, he went back to family life in Netherseal for the last time, still an Albion supporter to the end.

Jeff died at his daughter's home in Burton on Saturday January 19 2002. He was 59. The following day, before the First Division game between Albion and Walsall, a full house at The Hawthorns – and the millions who were watching at home, as *ITV* covered the game live — observed a minute's silence for the King. Thirteen weeks later, Jeff's beloved Albion beat Crystal Palace, and, at long last, returned to the top level of English football, where Jeff had made his name – and won so many fans — three decades earlier. He would have been so proud.

JEFF'S REPRESENTATIVE GAMES

England 0 Young England 0

April 25 1969 (Stamford Bridge)

England: Bonetti (Chelsea), Knowles (Tottenham), McNab (Arsenal), Mullery (Tottenham), McGrath (Southampton), Moore (West Ham), Sammells (Arsenal), Hurst (West Ham), Astle (WBA), Peters (West Ham), Tambling (Chelsea).

Young England: P Springett (Sheff Wed), Smith (Sheff Wed), Charles (West Ham), T Brown (WBA), McFarland (Derby), Hollins (Chelsea), Coates (Burnley), Robson (Newcastle), Weller (Millwall), Gould (Arsenal), Sissons (West Ham). Sub: George Armstrong (Arsenal) was substitute for BOTH sides!

England 2 Wales 1 *(Charlton, Lee)*

May 7 1969 (Wembley)

England: West (Everton), Newton (Blackburn), Cooper (Leeds), Moore (West Ham), J Charlton (Leeds), Hunter (Leeds), Lee (Man City), Bell (Man City), Astle (WBA), R Charlton (Man Utd), Ball (Everton) Att: 72,000

Mexico XI 0 England XI 4 *(Astle 2, Clarke 2)*

June 4 1969 (Guadalajara)

England XI: Shilton (Leicester), Wright (Everton), McNab (Arsenal), Harvey (Everton), J Charlton (Leeds), Moore (West Ham), Ball (Everton) [Mullery (Tottenham)], Bell (Man City), Astle (WBA), Clarke (Leicester), Peters (West Ham) [R Charlton (Man Utd)] Att: 48,000

England 1 Portugal 0 *(J Charlton)*

December 10 1969 (Wembley)

England: Bonetti (Chelsea), Reaney (Leeds), Hughes (Liverpool), Mullery (Tottenham), Moore (West Ham), J Charlton (Leeds), Lee (Man City), Bell (Man City) [Peters (West Ham)], Astle (WBA), R Charlton (Man Utd), Ball (Everton) Att: 100,000

Football League 3 Scottish League 2 *(Astle 2, Rogers)*

March 18 1970 (Highfield Road, Coventry)

Football League: Stepney (Man Utd) [Glazier (Coventry)], Smith (Liverpool), Hughes (Liverpool), Newton (Blackburn), McFarland (Derby), Todd (Sunderland), Coates (Burnley), Kidd (Man Utd) [Peters (Tottenham)], Astle (WBA), Harvey (Everton), Rogers (Swindon)

Columbia XI 0 England XI 1 *(Astle)*

May 20 1970

England XI: Bonetti (Chelsea, Wright (Everton), McNab (Arsenal), Hunter (Leeds), J Charlton (Leeds), Stiles (Man Utd), [Coates (Burnley)], Bell (Man City), Hughes (Liverpool), Kidd (Man Utd) [Astle (WBA)], Clarke (Leeds), Osgood (Chelsea)

Liga Univ 1 England XI 4 *(Astle 4)*

May 24 1970

England XI: Bonetti (Chelsea), Wright (Everton), Hughes (Liverpool), Stiles (Man Utd), J Charlton (Leeds), Hunter (Leeds), Osgood (Chelsea), Bell (Man City), Astle (WBA), Clarke (Leeds) [Coates (Burnley)], Thompson (Liverpool) [McNab (Arsenal)]

Brazil 1 England 0

June 7 1970 (Jalisco Stadium, Guadalajara)

England: Banks (Stoke), Wright (Everton), Cooper (Leeds), Mullery (Tottenham), Labone (Everton), Moore (West Ham), J Charlton (Leeds), Lee (Man City) [Astle (WBA)], Hurst (West Ham, Peters (Tottenham), R Charlton (Man Utd) [Bell (Man City)], Ball (Everton) Att: 66,750

England 1 Czechoslovakia 0 *(Clarke pen)*

June 11 1970 (Jalisco Stadium, Guadalajara)

England: Banks (Stoke), Newton (Everton), Cooper (Leeds), Mullery (Tottenham), Moore (West Ham), J Charlton (Leeds), Bell (Man City), Astle (WBA) [Osgood (Chelsea)], Clarke (Leeds), Peters (Tottenham), R Charlton (Man Utd) [Ball (Everton)] Att: 49,000

Irish League 0 Football League 5 *(Astle 2, Brown, Peters, Hector)*

(Carrow Road, Norwich) September 23 1970

Football League: Shilton (Leicester), Edwards (Man Utd) [D Smith (Stoke)], J Robson (Derby), Nish (Leicester), Sadler (Man Utd), Harvey (Everton), Coates (Burnley), Hector (Derby), Astle (WBA), Peters (Tottenham), Moore (Forest) [T Brown (WBA)]

Jeff's career appearances and goals for Albion, Albion Reserves and Notts County

	L	LC	FA	Eu	Tx	Wt	AI	Fr
1964-65	32(10)	0	1(1)	0	0	0	0	0
1965-66	27(18)	7(6)	0	0	0	0	0	10(1)
1966-67	38(16)	6(5)	2(1)	4	0	0	0	1
1967-68	40+1(26)	1	10(9)	0	0	0	0	8(5)
1968-69	37(21)	2(2)	5(2)	6(1)	0	0	0	1
1969-70	34(25)	9(5)	0	0	0	0	0	4(5)
1970-71	41(13)	3(1)	4(1)	0	2	0	3(1)	4(1)
1971-72	22(2)	0	0	0	0	3(2)	0	3
1972-73	14(5)	0	1	0	0	0	0	0
1973-74	5+1(1)	0	0	0	0	0	0	0
TOTALS	**290+2(137)**	**28(19)**	**23(14)**	**10(1)**	**2**	**3(2)**	**3(1)**	**31(12)**

ALBION RESERVES

	Central League
1964-65	0
1965-66	4 (3)
1966-67	1 (1)
1967-68	0
1968-69	0
1969-70	2 (2)
1970-71	0
1971-72	8 (4)
1972-73	7 (2)
1973-74	24 (10)
TOTAL	**46 (22)**

NOTTS COUNTY

	L	LC	FA
1961-62	7	0	1
1962-63	44(16)	2(3)	1
1963-64	41(11)	4(2)	3(1)
1964-65	11(4)	3(4)	0
TOTAL	**103(31)**	**9(9)**	**5(1)**

Abbreviations: L; League, LC; League Cup, FA: FA Cup, AI; Anglo-Italian Cup, Eu; Fairs Cup/ECWC, Tx; Texaco Cup, Wt; Watney Cup, Fr; friendlies

THE JEFF ASTLE ALBION GOAL COLLECTION

Below we record, match by match, every goal that Jeff scored for West Bromwich Albion, 1964-74. First figure listed is the goal time.

1964-65

Oct 10 1964 H Wolves 5-1
25: Kaye lobbed a clever ball forward for Astle to head his first ever Albion goal, despite the attention of two defenders
56: Astle collected a free kick from the left and eluded Graham Hawkins to fire past Showell in the Wolves goal
Oct 24 1964 H Liverpool 3-0
43: Hope sent a long ball through the Liverpool defence which Astle headed home, via the far post
Jan 9 1964 H Liverpool FAC 1-2
80: Astle pulled a goal back when he ran onto a Clive Clark header, slipped past Byrne and scored his first Albion Cup goal from close range
Feb 27 1965 H Aston Villa 3-1
55: Hope took the free kick after Pountney had handled, and Astle headed a great goal, despite Withers' acrobatic dive
Mar 13 1965 H Leicester 6-0
3: Banks, under pressure from Ray Crawford, cleared a Williams lob right to the feet of Astle, who placed the ball home with great skill
76: Astle rounded off the drubbing of Leicester when he ghosted in to head home a Hope centre
Mar 23 1965 H Everton 4-0
48: Harris failed to control a long Williams pass down the touchline, and Astle scored with a long range drive that went in off the underside of the bar
75: Albion went two up when Astle was played on-side by a touch by an Everton defender, from another Williams long ball, and he coolly slipped the ball home.
Apr 16 1965 A West Ham 1-6
45: After getting a first half drubbing, Albion were fortunate to be only 2-1 down at the break, when Astle scored with a shot that went in off two defenders
Apr 19 1965 H West Ham 4-2
13: Astle headed in an inswinging Hope corner to put Albion two up against the team he most liked scoring against

1965-66

Aug 21 1965 H West Ham 3-0
37: On the opening day of the 1965-66 season, Albion got off to a great start, Astle scoring their second goal when he took a perfect pass down the middle from Fraser to beat Standen with a fine shot
Aug 28 1965 A Nottingham F 2-3
8: Astle headed home a Hope cross to open the score in a game in which Albion would throw away a two goal lead
Sep 4 1965 H Sheff Wed 4-2
4: Ken Foggo went on a great wing run and crossed for Astle to head home
44: Another Foggo cross, another Astle header to make it 2-2 at half time
46: A great goal. Astle fed Kaye, who supplied Clark to cross for Astle to race in and crack the ball home from the winger's reverse pass, for the centre-forward's first hat-trick
Sep 7 1965 A Everton 3-2
70: Astle went to the top of the First Division scoring charts when he scored the winner against third-placed Everton, with a great header from Ken Foggo's right wing corner
Sep 10 1965 A Northampton 4-3
11: Albion put Albion two up in their first League visit to Northampton when he nudged home a close range effort from Foggo's cross

54: Kaye supplied Tony Brown, who put in a quick cross for Astle to shoot past Harvey

67: Astle made it two hat-tricks in the space of seven days when he scored a tremendous header from a Kaye centre

Sep 15 1965 H Everton 1-1

70: Brown put Astle through, swapping passes with Lovett before taking advantage of Labone's slip to fire home a ground shot into the corner

Oct 13 1965 A Leeds Utd LC 4-2

20: A great three man move involving Kaye and Clark was rounded off when Astle blasted past Harvey

Oct 16 1965 A Aston Villa 1-1

79: The home side dominated the first half, Albion the second, and Astle headed a great cross from Brown over the badly placed Withers

Nov 10 1965 H Coventry LC 6-1

1: Forty seconds into the League Cup replay a glorious Hope pass was cleared to Fairfax, who crossed for Astle to drive home from the edge of the box

58: A classic Astle header from Clark's cross, despite being fouled by Curtis

77: Another great Astle header to complete his third hat-trick for the club.

Dec 1 1965 H Peterborough LC 2-1

38: Astle gave Albion the lead in this League Cup semi-final first leg, when he scored from close range after John Kaye lobbed through a Hope centre

Feb 9 1965 A West Ham LC 1-2

59: A vital opening goal in the first leg of the League Cup Final at Upton Park, Astle meeting a Clive Clark cross with a glorious right foot shot

Apr 2 1966 A Fulham 1-2

22: A simple tap-in at Craven Cottage to equalise an early goal from Haynes

Apr 11 1966 H Arsenal 4-4

66: Four goals to one down after 64 minutes, Astle kindled the revival when he blazed a Fraser cross past Furnell

Apr 16 1966 A Blackburn 1-0

84: Astle ran onto a Tony Brown pass, drew Else and rolled the ball home – the goal relegated luckless Rovers to Division Two for 25 years

Apr 22 1966 H Leicester 5-1

41: Astle had a hand in all five goals in a brilliant display; his goal came when the striker forced a Clive Clark cross over the line.

Apr 25 1966 A Chelsea 3-2

4: Astle headed a Hope corner in off Bonetti's body to put the Albion two up.

76: A simple close-range effort from Clark's cross to win the game

May 7 1966 H Tottenham 2-1

27: Cram sent Fraser away, and his centre was perfect, Astle just beating goalkeeper Brown to the ball to score his 18th goal of the season, making him Albion's top scorer for the first time

1966-67

Aug 24 1966 A Leeds Utd 1-2

31: Astle pulled a goal back at Elland Road when Clark headed down Fairfax's free kick, Kaye hit the bar and Astle touched in the rebound

Sep 10 1966 H Fulham 5-1

54: After a slow first half, Albion started a rout when Clark beat Cohen and crossed for the King to ram home from eight yards

Sep 17 1966 A Everton 4-5

7: Astle started the scoring in an amazing game at Goodison, when he headed in a Cram centre

Oct 1 1966 A Sheffield Utd 3-4

8: Another high scoring thriller, with Albion again taking an early lead when Astle shot home at the end of a slick Albion move.

Oct 5 1966 H Manchester City LC 4-2

62: A typical Astle trademark header from a Hope corner

Oct 15 1966 H Aston Villa 2-1
15: Withers failed to cut out a Krzywicki centre and the ball bounced off the bar onto the head of Astle, who made no mistake
Oct 25 1966 A Swindon T LC 2-0
83: Seven minutes from the end of a tense League Cup tie, the holders went through to the fifth round when Astle scored with a superb floated header from a Crawford cross
Oct 29 1966 H Sheffield Wed 1-2
59: Astle scored Albion's equaliser when he harassed Wednesday goalkeeper Springett into dropping the ball, then simply tapped it into the net
Dec 17 1966 H Manchester Utd 3-4
7: After a long spell out with injury, Astle outjumped the United defence to head a picture equaliser to Herd's earlier goal
43: Astle pulled a goal back to make it 3-4 at the break with another spectacular headed goal from a Hope cross, in this Hawthorns goal feast
Dec 31 1966 A Burnley 1-5
82: Five goals down at Turf Moor, Astle headed a late goal from a cross from Kenny Stephens
Jan 18 1967 H West Ham LC 4-0
1: After just 50 seconds Collard crossed from the left and Astle outjumped Ken Brown to head magnificently past Standen
24: Kaye's shot was blocked by a defender, Astle followed up to fire home his second
44: After having had two more goals disallowed, Astle completed his hat-trick on the stroke of half time when he beat two defenders to drive in from ten yards
Jan 28 1967 A Northampton FAC 3-1
9: Astle fastened onto a long pass from Bobby Hope to send in an unstoppable first time shot in what was their second visit to the County Ground that season
Feb 4 1967 A Stoke 1-1
79: A simple tap over the line after keeper John Farmer had fumbled Kaye's dipping centre
Feb 25 1967 H Sunderland 2-2
86: Tony Brown crossed from the right and Astle headed an equaliser off the inside of the right post
Mar 27 1967 H Southampton 3-2
67: Saints goalkeeper Eric Martin failed to cut out Foggo's cross, allowing Astle to send a header just inside the far post to put Albion 3-1 ahead in a vital relegation match
Mar 28 1967 A Southampton 2-2
22: The following day Astle put Albion ahead at the Dell when he ran through to volley home a Hope pass, with the home defence waiting for an offside flag
Apr 22 1967 A Liverpool 1-0
64: Liverpool's first home defeat for two years – Astle's goal, from a bad back pass from Yates, which Jeff picked up to beat Lawrence gave Albion the two points they needed to stave off relegation, and end Liverpool's hopes of the title.
Apr 28 1967 H West Ham 3-1
76: A classic power header from a Bobby Hope free kick that put Albion three up
May 6 1967 A Blackpool 3-1
60: Astle equalised against already relegated Blackpool when he intercepted Green's poor clearance from a Clark cross, and picked his spot to beat Thomas

1967-68

Aug 30 1967 H Wolves 4-1
11: Albion took the lead when Phil Parkes could only push out a Tony Brown shot to the feet of Astle, who slammed the loose ball into the net
Sep 23 1967 A Coventry 2-4
9: Stephens curled in a great cross and Astle fired Albion into an early lead with a half-volley that went in off the crossbar at Highfield Road in the first League meeting between the two clubs
Sep 30 1967 H Sheff Utd 4-1
6: Astle slammed home the rebound after Clark had misdirected his header from Hope's centre.

29: Another glorious Hope pass sent Stephens away,and when he pulled the ball back, Astle headed past Hodgkinson

78: A fourth hat-trick for Astle when he fired home the rebound after Clark's shot had cannoned back off the goalkeeper

Oct 7 1967 A Fulham 2-1

34: Clive Clark beat both Dempsey and Callaghan and put over a low cross which Hope touched on for Astle to crash home

Oct 14 1967 H Leeds Utd 2-0

14: A great win against a Leeds side that had scored 19 goal in their previous three games; Astle glided a header past Sprake from Brown's long free kick

68: Astle ran onto a Brown through ball to shoot home his second goal

Nov 11 1967 H Burnley 8-1

75: From a Kaye cross, Astle sent in a fine shot that swerved away from Thomson for Albion's eighth

Nov 18 1967 A Sheff Wed 2-2

85: On a foggy and frosty day, Astle salvaged a point at Hillsborough when Fraser went past Don Megson and Astle sent in a gliding header from the back's great cross

Dec 11 1967 A West Ham 3-2

78: A great left wing cross from Hope gave Astle the opportunity to head home

Dec 16 1967 A Chelsea 3-0

76: Astle ran onto a loose ball in the Chelsea defence to fire in a left footer from the edge of the box

Dec 26 1967 H Manchester City 3-2

27: A copybook Astle header from Hope's precise corner kick

89: Hope's long cross found Tony Brown, who slipped the ball inside for Astle to fire home the winner against the eventual First Division champions

Jan 31 1968 H Colchester FAC 4-0

16: Astle clipped home first time a Fraser cross, after the left half had been sent away by Hope; his first goal in a historic FA Cup sequence

Feb 10 1968 A Sheffield Utd 1-1

25: Kaye sent Hartford away and the youngster put in a quick and accurate centre for Astle to run in between two defenders to steer the ball past Hodgkinson

Feb 21 1968 A Southampton FAC 3-2

16: Astle chested down Hope's cross and pushed the ball past Martin to level in an epic cup tie

90: Lovett shot against the post; the ball rebounded out wide to Clark, who put over a low cross for Astle to slam home a last minute winner against all the odds. Cup goals number two and three

Feb 24 1968 H Fulham 2-1

14: A Hope pass split the Fulham defence side open, for Astle to race through

Mar 9 1968 A Portsmouth FAC 2-1

29: Hope put over another precision free kick for Astle to head the opening salvo of a bad-tempered cup tie. Cup goal number four

Mar 13 1968 H Stoke City 3-0

70: In the absence of Tony Brown, Astle stepped up to beat Gordon Banks from the penalty spot after Lovett had been brought down

90: A great goal, as Astle ran through down the middle on his own, sent Banks the wrong way, and slipped the ball into an empty net

Mar 23 1968 A Leicester 3-2

83: Albion came back from a two goal deficit, thanks to two strikes from Clive Clark. The winger went through for his hat-trick, but Shilton parried and Astle to steered home the winner

Apr 8 1968 A Liverpool FAC 1-1

67: Fraser supplied Tony Brown who beat his man before crossing left footed for Astle to head wide of the diving Lawrence. Cup goal number five

Apr 13 1968 H Sheff Wed 1-1

44: Ronnie Rees was fouled by Smith just outside the area; Rees took the free kick and Astle darted in to steer a header just inside the near post

152

Apr 18 1968 N Liverpool FAC 2-1
7: Jeff raced away down the left to score with a drive inside the near post.

Apr 27 1968 N Birmingham FAC 2-0
13: Winston Foster was penalised for a foul on Astle, 30 yards out. Brown touched the free kick to Hope, and Herriott did well to save, but Astle placed an angled shot into the empty net from the rebound. Cup goal number seven

Apr 29 1968 H Manchester Utd 6-3
9: Tony Dunne put the ball straight to Astle in the box, and he beat a challenge by Denis Law to shoot home left-footed
59: A perfect cross from a free kick on the left from Hope for Astle to head Albion 4-0 up, the ball going through Stepney's arms
70: Astle completed his fifth hat-trick with another great header, from Lovett's right wing cross

May 1 1968 H West Ham 3-1
28: Astle rose magnificently above Cushley to head home Bobby Hope's well placed corner kick
36: Asa Hartford crossed a long ball into the middle and once again Astle outjumped Cushley to score with another great header
55: Jeff completed his second hat-trick in three days when Cushley failed to clear a Hope cross, and Astle zipped in to steer the ball past Ferguson

May 18 1968 H Everton FAC 1-0
93: Jeff's most memorable goal. He fired in a right footer from the edge of the box, and then, as the ball rebounded back to him from a defender'' backside, he lashed the ball into the top corner with his left foot. "He probably never scored another left footer" – Bobby Hope

1968-69

Aug 14 1968 H Manchester Utd 3-1
4: It looked like a repeat of the previous season's 6-3 when Williams crossed for Astle to head home another early goal against the champions of Europe
18: Williams chipped the ball into the United box, and when the visitors defence was all at sixes and sevens, Astle headed home as Foulkes waited for Stepney to collect

Aug 21 1968 A Tottenham 1-1
70: Astle climbed high to beat Mike England to a high Brown cross, to delicately glance an equaliser past Jennings

Aug 24 1968 H Burnley 3-2
44: Graham Williams swept the perfect centre in at the near post where Astle left Thomson helpless with the perfect back header
84: Thomson could only parry a Rees shot and Astle pounced to fire home.

Sep 3 1968 N Nottingham F LC 3-2
30: Back on his "home" ground at Meadow Lane, Astle opened the scoring when he poked home a quick pass from Tony Brown
57: Albion went 3-1 when Hope crossed for the unmarked Astle to head past Brian Williamson

Sep 7 1968 H Nottingham F 2-5
55: Tony Brown made all the running; when his shot bounced back off McKinlay, Astle blasted home from close range

Sep 14 1968 A Newcastle 3-2
16: Harassed by Hartford, Burton failed to clear properly and Astle had all the time in the world to whip the ball into the net
58: Hope sent in a long free kick and Astle ran forward to score with a glorious diving header

Oct 5 1968 H QPR 3-1
43: A great header from the edge of the box from Hartford's cross.

Oct 9 1968 H Coventry 6-1
51: A high Rees cross was pushed out to Astle on the edge of the box,a nd he sent in a fine drive which Glazier touched, but could not stop
75: Tudor made a terrible hash of trying to clear a Hartford cross and Astle nipped in to tap home

Oct 12 1968 A Leicester 2-0
9: From a long Talbut clearance, Astle forced Manley into a hurried back pass, rounded Shilton, and walked the ball home
Nov 27 1968 H D Bucharest ECWC 4-0
72: Astle scored his first goal in seven weeks when he ran in a Hope pass to put Albion three up against the Rumanians
Jań 4 1969 H Norwich FAC 3-0
48: When Mallender handled a Hope cross, in the absence of Tony Brown, Jeff Astle scored a rare penalty, blasting low and hard past Keelan
Feb 1 1969 A Stoke City 1-1
90: Tony ran unchallenged for 30 yards, and when the ball ran loose, Astle poked home a last minute goal from the melee that Albion did not really deserve
Mar 1 1969 A Chelsea FAC 2-1
59: Tony Brown crossed from the right, Astle collected and fired past Bonetti, who got his hands to the ball, to book Albion a place in their second consecutive FA Cup semi-final
Apr 2 1969 A Manchester Utd 1-2
53: A great goal at Old Trafford. Astle collected a 40 yard Hope pass, dummied two defenders, then scored right footed from an impossible angle, the ball just creeping inside the far post
Apr 5 1969 H Everton 1-1
40: Krzywicki ran onto a great Hope through ball; he shot for goal, but as the ball was passing wide, Jeff ran in to push it into the net at the far post
Apr 7 1969 H Tottenham 4-3
51: Astle pulled a goal back for Albion when he flicked home a Lovett through ball
69: Astle charged onto Krzywicki's right wing cross to hammer Albion's winner from close range – his 22nd goal of the season
Apr 14 1969 H West Ham 3-1
65: A lucky goal. Bobby Ferguson's goal kick hit Jeff on the back of his head as he was walking back to the centre; he turned, move to the edge of the area, and fired home a vicious drive
70: Kaye sent Hope away, and he chipped the ball in for Astle to head into the net at the far post
Apr 19 1969 H Newcastle 5-1
77: Hartford fed Tony Brown, who slipped the ball through for Astle to score Albion's fifth goal with an angled drive
Apr 23 1969 H Ipswich T 2-2
56: Lovett put over a right wing cross and Astle flung himself at the ball

1969-70

Sep 3 1969 A Aston Villa LC 2-1
77: Six minutes after Villa had levelled, Tony Brown shot against the bar and Astle ran on to score with a stooping header from the rebound, before celebrating in front of the Holte End
Sep 13 1969 H Ipswich 2-2
23: Kaye put in a long free kick and Astle outjumped Best to head into the corner
51: Hartford sent Astle clear with a brilliant through ball which allowed the striker to beat Best
Sep 17 1969 H Stoke 1-3
39: Astle shrugged off a heavy challenge from Denis Smith to force Krzywicki's pass past Banks
Sep 20 1969 A Crystal P 3-1
44: Hegan, Brown and Suggett all combined to cross for Astle to force a way past McCormick to put Albion three up in their first ever League meeting with Palace
Sep 27 1969 H Liverpool 2-2
4: Hegan won a tackle on the halfway line, fed Brown, who inter-passed with Astle, who blasted the ball past Lawrence
Oct 1 1969 H Ipswich T LC 2-0
67: A defence-splitting pass from Hegan sent Krzywicki away, and he beat a defender before laying the ball off for Astle to score with an angled shot

Oct 7 1969 A Arsenal 1-1
4: Krzywicki forced a corner, well placed by Hope, for Astle to head spectacularly home, despite the attentions of several Arsenal defenders
Oct 11 1969 H Leeds Utd 1-1
27: Hope swept the ball across from the right for Astle to run into the net against the champions
Nov 5 1969 H Leicester City LC 2-1
15: Fraser crossed from the right, Suggett headed straight at Shilton, and when the young keeper failed to gather properly, Astle was there to bundle the ball in.
21: Astle headed down to Hope, and when Shilton parried the Scotsman's fierce shot, Astle was there again, first to the rebound
Nov 8 1969 H Everton 2-0
25: A superb left foot volley after Fraser had lobbed a free kick 40 yards to Astle's feet
Nov 22 1969 H Sheff Wed 3-0
72: Hartford slammed a tremendous shot against the bar, and Astle was in like a flash to score from the rebound; his 100th League goal for the Albion
Dec 13 1969 A Ipswich T 1-0
68: After Dennis Martin had challenged for a Kaye free kick Astle rammed the loose ball past Best. Albion would not win another away match for over a year
Dec 26 1969 H West Ham 3-1
60: Astle flicked in a header after Ferguson had failed to cut out Hope's corner kick
Jan 10 1970 H Crystal P 3-2
36: Astle equalised for Albion with a beautiful shot on the turn from the edge of the area
41: Hope gave the ball to Astle in a crowded goalmouth and he scored with a quick snap-shot
79: Suggett dived to head on a Hope cross and the ball fell nicely for Astle to fire home to complete what would be the last Albion hat-trick of his career
Jan 28 1970 H Sunderland 3-1
37: Fraser moved the ball out of defence, Hartford put it through for Suggett to flick on, and Astle calmly steered the ball past Montgomery
87: Astle finished off a precision pass from Bobby Hope
Jan 31 1970 H Man City 3-0
30: Tony Brown made a quick break down the centre and Astle quickly controlled his pass to drive the ball past Mulhearn
Feb 10 1970 A Leeds Utd 1-5
26: Ray Wilson made an excursion into the Leeds area, Sprake could only parry, and Astle picked up the rebound
Feb 28 1970 H Wolves 3-3
25: After Brown's free kick had been cleared, Cantello returned the ball, Astle headed down, and when Suggett gave him the ball back, he scored with a first time angled shot
Mar 7 1970 N Man City LC 1-2
5: A high, lofted ball from the left from full-back Ray Wilson, and Astle beat Corrigan in the air to head a classic goal.
Mar 14 1970 H Newcastle 2-2
31: Tony Brown's free kick was blocked by a Newcastle defender, and Astle pounced on the rebound to equalise
52: Astle scored with a close range effort after Suggett's shot had cannoned back off a defender
Mar 28 1970 H Tottenham 1-1
68: A beautiful right-footed curler which beat Jennings after he had run onto a pass from Brown
Mar 30 1970 H Chelsea 3-1
48: Bobby Hope crossed from the right for Astle to head past Bonetti
Apr 4 1970 H Nottngham F 4-0
45: In injury time, Suggett sent Allan Glover away to cross for Astle to head inside the far post
Apr 15 1970 A Stoke City 2-3
1: An amazing goal, scored after just fifteen seconds. Jeff kicked off to Hartford, and raced

upfield for the return ball. When it reached him, he tried an ambitious overhead kick, which caught Gordon Banks off his line, to bounce over his head and into the net for Astle's 30th goal of the season

1970-71

Aug 18 1970 A Nottingham F 3-3
88: A late, late equaliser at the City Ground, as Astle stole up on the blind side to convert Tony Brown's right wing corner
Aug 22 1970 A Blackpool 1-3
2: Hope sent Cantello into space on the left and his centre gave Astle a tap-in at the far post
Aug 26 1970 H Stoke City 5-2
2: Another early goal. Astle blocked Banks' drop-kick with his backside, waltzed around his England colleague, and tapped home
89: Suggett raced down the right to lay on a perfect pass for Astle to glide the ball past Banks at the far post to seal a great win
Aug 29 1970 H Liverpool 1-1
79: Tony Brown picked up on a Tommy Smith error just outside the area to set up Astle to blast home a deserved equaliser
Sep 2 1970 H Newcastle 1-2
14: New signing from Carlisle, George McVitie, beat two men and crossed from the right for Astle to score his first header of the season at the near post
Sep 8 1970 H Charlton LC 3-1
16: Astle picked up a rebound to fire home a right footed drive, off the bar, from an acute angle
Oct 3 1970 A Ipswich T 2-2
48: Astle raced in to blast home Tony Brown's low cross, to complete a comeback from two down
Oct 31 1970 H Everton 3-0
26: McVitie headed down Suggett's cross for Astle to turn on a sixpence and jab home from ten yards
Nov 28 1970 H Chelsea 2-2
65: Brown's left wing cross found Astle, who forced the ball in from six yards
Jan 11 1971 A Scunthorpe FAC 3-1
64: Jeff completed a good second half comeback for Albion at the Old Show Ground, when he headed on a Lovett cross from the right to Brown,took the return, and shot low into the corner
Jan 30 1971 A Chelsea 1-4
25: Hartford forced a way through on the left, crossing low for Astle to turn the ball in from six yards
Feb 27 1971 A Everton 3-3
6: Wile headed down Hope's corner, Hartford chipped in and Astle headed a fine goal after a well-timed run that foxed Kenyon
Apr 9 1971 A West Ham 1-2
30: Tony Brown's shot rebounded off Ferguson, straight to Astle, who lunged forward to head into an empty net
Apr 17 1971 A Leeds Utd 2-1
69: The most controversial goal of Jeff's career; a simple tap in from six yards, from Tony's pass, but Jeff looked to be offside as he scored the goal that helped to destroy Leeds' title hopes
May 29 1971 H Cagliari AIC 1-2
80: Astle equalised against the Italians with an easy goal after goalkeeper Albertosi pushed out Ray Wilson's shot right to his feet

1971-72

Aug 7 1971 H Colchester WC 4-4
29: Gilchrist's attempted clearance hit a team mate and dropped to the feet of Astle, who turned the ball into the net past Graham Smith
89: Suggett's corner produced a scramble in the area, and Astle turned the ball home to force a draw and a penalty shoot-out

Nov 13 1971 A Nottingham F 1-4
22: In his first back after a long spell out injured, Astle scored from the rebound after Barron had saved Tony Brown's shot
Jan 29 1972 H Manchester Utd 2-1
77: A great Asa Hartford volley, from a "trick" free kick, bounced off the bar for Astle to score with a header

1972-73

Mar 3 1972 A Manchester Utd 1-2
40: A crucial relegation tussle. Hartford intercepted a Charlton pass and fed Tony Brown, who back-heeled the ball for Astle to fire a delightful volley which spun out of Stepney's hands and over the line
Apr 7 1972 H Leicester 1-0
27: Roger Minton's long free kick reached Tony Brown; he tried a cross-shot and the rebound bounced up for Astle to score a vital goal from an acute angle
Apr 11 1972 H Everton 4-1
26: A snapshot which lawson should have saved, but the young keeper allowed the ball to slip through his hands
Apr 25 1972 H Manchester City 1-2
54: Alan Merrick crossed from the left, Wile challenged Healey, and when the ball dropped, Astle was there to bang it home for the equaliser, in a game that Albion had to win to avoid relegation
Apr 28 1972 A Birmingham 2-3
40: Cantello and Hartford completely wrong-footed the Blues defence and laid on a simple goal for Astle; his last at the top level

1973-74

Feb 23 1973 H Bristol C 2-2
70: Asa Hartford made a square run on the right, before chipping in delightfully onto the head of Astle, who got up well to head past Cashley, before being lost in a swarm of young fans. His last goal for the Albion.

In all, Jeff scored 174 competitive goals for the Albion: 137 in the League, 19 in the League Cup, 14 FA Cup, 1 ECWC, 1 Anglo-Italian and 2 Watney Cup. He also scored another 12 goals in friendlies/tour matches and Testimonial games (see below)

July 11 1966	N Ferencvaros (NYC)	1-1
Aug 7 1967	A Bristol C (Fr)	4-1
Aug 12 1967	A Portsmouth (Fr)	1-0
May 23 1968	N Dar-es-Salaam (Fr)	1-1
May 25 1968	N Tanzania (Fr)	1-1
Jun 5 1968	N East Africa (Fr)	2-2
July 31 1968	A SKL Oslo (Fr)	6-0 (3 goals)
July 26 1969	A Rotherham (Fr)	4-0
Jan 23 1970	A Birmingham (Fr)	2-2
May 18 1971	A Swansea (Testimonial)	2-2

For Notts County Jeff scored 31 League goals, plus 9 in the League Cup and 1 in the FA Cup.

FRIENDS OF JEFF ASTLE

001	John Homer	046	Dave Walker
002	Sarah-Jane Homer	047	Andrew Saunders
003	David Thomas Homer	048	Graham Belt
004	Dave Holloway	049	Ashley Hayward
005	Vicki Ashfield	050	Ray Kemp
006	Joan Willmore	051	Roger Hill
007	Valerie Willmore	052	Tony Turner
008	Kevin Grice	053	Paul Johnson
009		054	Ken Spencer
010	Dorothy Ingram	055	Clive Smith
011	Karen Wright	056	Clive Blake
012	Richard Brennan	057	Mark A Whitehouse
013	Steve Waterhouse	058	Michael Baxter
014	Mark Bell	059	Leslie Thompson
015	Allan Timmins	060	James Simcox
016	Steve Cannon	061	Graham Hartill
017	Paul Ellis	062	B P Turner
018	Peter Hall	063	Gary Knapman
019	Ian D Glen	064	Paul Murray
020	Dave Fryer	065	Paul Harrison
021	Julian Rowe	066	Alan G Smith
022	Paul Collins	067	Ron Worley
023	Andy Croydon	068	David Kendrick
024	Richard Jones	069	John Houghton
025	Robert Aiken	070	Chris Holt
026	Dougie Webb	071	Liam Ballantine
027	Richard Crump	072	Phil Surridge (IOW)
028	Lynda Cooper	073	Chris Dawson
029	Mrs G A McNeill	074	Kevin Rhodes
030	Brian Simcox	075	Keith L Melhuish
031	Trevor Challoner	076	John Woffinden
032	Peter Baxendale	077	John A Castle
033	G J Wheeler	078	Martin Bullock
034	Brian Kirkham	079	David Thorne
035	Ian Hoult	080	Neil Reynolds
036	Laura Hoult	081	Charlie Reynolds
037	R Priest	082	Brian Cooper
038	Andy Wilce	083	Richard Barton
039	Ken Smith	084	Jody Kant
040	Derek Tudor	085	Amanda Palfrey
041	Reg Snell	086	Ted Smith
042	Helen Moore	087	Jeff Prestridge
043	June Moore	088	Bill Spencer
044	Mike Phipps	089	Carlos The Jackal Diaz
045	Maurice M Leyland	090	Graeme Burdon

091	N M Stokes
092	Adrian Dudley-Evans
093	David Vine
094	Paul Homer
095	Wayne Fisher
096	S J Dangerfield
097	Janice Taylor
098	Paul Roberts
099	Steve Tongue
100	Oliver Willmore
101	Alan Wheatley
102	David Russell
103	Dean Walton
104	A M Rogers
105	M J Edwards
106	Stephen Crees
107	Les Woodhall
108	Mike Westwood
109	Brian Androlia
110	Mr D A Mills
111	John Griffin
112	Peter Gregory
113	Trevor Crewe
114	John Burke
115	D E Holyhead
116	Kevin Smyth
117	W D Ellis
118	John Milton
119	Russell Cooper
120	G J Greenhough
121	Steve Mole
122	Mike Buckland
123	J Byrne
124	Tony Matthews
125	Terry Wills
126	D R Sharpe
127	S Brookes
128	Colin Jones
129	Gareth Palmer Jones
130	Robert Sheppard
131	Steve Matthews
132	Alan Ison
133	Bill Young
134	Olivia Young
135	Robert Young

136	Mark+David Swallow	187	Garth Wooldridge	238	Gary Ross
137	Laura+Jack Swallow	188	Ann Wooldridge	239	Gaynor Thornton
138	Sarah Swallow	189	Mrs S Cutler	240	Andy Price
139	Gail Crawford	190	Sarah+Joseph Cutler	241	P J Evans
140	Alan Phillips	191	Sophie Cutler	242	D C Evans
141	T B Baxter	192	James R Cartwright	243	Andrew Miller
142	Ami Batham	193	A J Timmins	244	Kevin Horton
143	Emily Batham	194	David Sheppard	245	Nigel Pritchard
144	R D Martin	195	Geoff A Whitehouse	246	Bernard Dowell
145	Keith Wibberley	196	Ian Boswell	247	Robert Frank Dale
146	David Knowlton	197	Chris Purdon	248	Anthony Hopkins
147	Mark Castle	198	Carl Harris	249	Brian Mulcahy
148	Cliff Price	199	Simon Flower	250	Ian John Richards
149	Trevor M Davenport	200	Allan Maull	251	Robert Higgins
150	C D Bell	201	Helen Maull	252	Moray Allan
151	Andrew Byrne	202	Anthony J Curtis	253	Christopher Hall
152	David Byrne	203	Cavan Timmins	254	R Morris
153	Duncan Chadwick	204	Roy Kinsey	255	John Murphy
154	P S W Jeremy	205	Richard Hill	256	Chris Marsh
155	Steve Carr	206	Mel Turner	257	Alan Hobson
146	Garry D Elwell	207	Darren Cooper	258	Eric Hobson
157	Robert G Elwell	208	Martin Banner	259	June Platt
158	Peter J Elwell	209	Keith Fisher	260	Martin Foster
159	Elaine S Elwell	210	Robert Fisher	261	Clive Buckland
160	Lew Clews	211	John Gaughey	262	Chris Foxall
161	Bob Macvie	212	Colin Blount	263	Greg Lander
162	Mark Skellon	213	Jonathan Slim	264	Andrew Masters
163	Peter Wall	214	Graham Smyth	265	Jim French
164	Simon Wall	215	Spiro Marcetic	266	Alan Jones
165	David Howson	216	George Prest	267	David Jones
166	Dave Williams	217	David Perkins	268	Gary Hyde
167	Di Williams	218	S A Moss	269	J E Osborne
168	Barry Brisland	219	James Meighan	270	Bruce Allison
169	Andrew Saunders	220	Roland Meighan	271	Sean Willis
170	Alan Hughes	221	Graeme Parsons	272	Brian Willis
171	Robin Dobin Thomas	222	John O'Brien	273	Ian Tubby
172	I J van der Werff	223	Anthony Flynn	274	Søren Jensen
173	P S J Robottom	224	Paul Bennett	275	Terry Davies
174	Stephen Hyde	225	Robin A B Viner	276	Jonathan Hillier
175	Roy Walford	226	Robert Bradley	277	Philip Shaw
176	D H Jennings	227	Michael Thomas	278	Mark Gullick
177	Jonathan Want	228	J Hassell	279	E Mooney
178	Mick Corfield	229	Mick Brown	280	James Haynes
179	**Wally Henvey RIP**	230	Dennis Harwood	281	T Cook (Cookie)
180	Janet Cotterill	231	A R Bosworth	282	Derek Wardell
181	Alan Cotterill	232	Tim Watson	283	Mark Pearsall
182	J Smallwood	233	Alan Lowndes	284	Steve Finn
183	R Harman	234	Nick Fletcher	285	Linda Millard
184	David Valder	235	Giancarlo 'Giano' Casci	286	Roy Bradshaw
185	Guy Smith	236	Reijo Lampinen	287	Phillip Taylor
186	Janet Rayner	237	Kayley Humble	288	Matthew Taylor

289	D Brown	340	John R Jones	391	Archie Ryan
290	Baz+Rob Jones	341	Bryn Jones	392	Roger Fallon
291	Mike Tilt	342	John Rowe	393	Tony Parris
292	Andrew Shingleton	343	Paula Beardsmore	394	Allister Collings
293	Geoff Lawday	344	Chris Flanagan	395	Cathy+John Maddox
294	Paul Foster	345	Jeff Prestridge	396	Neil Burns
295	P W K Rathkey	346	Steve Grice	397	Terry Hill
296	T K O'Connell	347	Andy Heselgrove	398	Spencer Smith
297	Leonard Green	348	Mel Greenfield	399	David Warner
298	A Atkinson	349	Kevin Hadley	400	Keith A Simcox
299	Peter Knowles	350	Martin Dawes	401	Martin Brown
300	J Blakesley	351	Philip Metcalfe	402	Fred R Jones
301	L A Fletcher	352	P A Burford	403	Robert Kingston
302	Dave Wright	353	Andrew Saunders	404	Dan Dale
303	M Wilson	354	Dennis Rose	405	Rod Burton
304	Steve Morris	355	Jason Dennis Rose	406	Colin Mackenzie
305	Sophie Morris	356	Dave Justin Rose	407	David Bending
306	Ellie Morris	357	Stephen McGreevy	408	David Grigg
307	Jayne Gazey	358	Chris Cadman	409	Ronnie Grigg
308	Rebecca Gazey	359	Peter Grimley	410	Brian Hopkins
309	Alan Love	360	Darryl Thomas	411	Barry Shermer
310	Mr N Hathaway	361	Robert L Mills	412	Peter Moore
311	Margaret Hickman	362	Gordon Carswell	413	Martyn Ridout
312	David R Woodward	363	Nigel Woodall	414	Adam Siniarski
313	Jonathan Eden	364	Clive Hansell	415	David Royce
314	Verity Eden	365	Mark Williams	416	Patrick Benton
315	Thomas Northall	366	John Fox	417	Julie Fulwell
316	Mick+June Northall	367	Steve Jervis	418	Matthew Bytheway
317	Mark Ralphs	368	John Barnes	419	Greg Bevin
318	Kelvin Rzepkowski	369	Kevin Pendrey	420	John Green
319	Peter Coleman	370	Paul Wood	421	Ron W Williams
320	Rob Robbins	371	Jeff Powell	422	Doreen Brookes
321	Martin Chatwin	372	John (Sooty) Sutton	423	Richard Bastable
322	Leanne Farrington	373	Mark Colley	424	B R Evans
323	John Farrington	374	Clint Harrison	425	Mick Ratcliffe
324	John Whitton	375	John K Powell	426	Graham Cresswell
325	Hilary Boddy	376	Marie Lilly	427	Steve Williams
326	Dean Paul Bamford	377	Steve Dingley	428	Ben Hall
327	Pete Edwards	378	Paul Kent	429	Kevin Morris
328	Peter Lunn	379	Craig Towns	430	Frank Taylor. Organford
329	Roger Stubbs	380	Anita Towns	431	G I F Godby
330	Kevin Witten	381	Deb Longhurst	432	I P F Godby
331	William Harris	382	Sean Longhurst	433	Michael & Paul Faulkner
332	J L R Walker	383	Ryan Carpenter	434	Brian Kite
333	Vince Barber	384	Peter Turner	435	Jules Kite-Lightfoot
334	J Houghton	385	Richard Mountford*	436	Jacq Walker
335	Tony Kenny	386	Roy Haden	437	Nigel Waters
336	Gerry Kenny	387	Jack Cheshire	438	Dean Fletcher
337	Stephen Orr	388	Alan Cleverley	439	Darren Somers
338	Mick Bryan	389	Geoff Nevey	440	John Whitehouse
339	Peter Stockton	390	Brian John Dearn	441	Ian J Wright